"Part epistolary memoir and part emotive taxonomy of significant flora and fauna, the primary endeavor of this book, Taranto's debut, is transformation: to wring from grief the shape and substance of art."

—PUBLISHERS WEEKLY

"An unusual narrative of loss that becomes both a meditation on the Earth and a benediction for one who won't be around to enjoy it. Taranto's first book is a poetic memoir steeped in beginnings and endings **GULF GATE PUBLIC LIBRARY** t at resolving a person sideration of how thi

"*Ars Botanica* is a gorgeous hybrid: a memoir in letters to a phantom addressee, an introduction to life on this planet, a primer for how to live, a meditation on family. It also winds up being a beautiful and highly personal field guide to the natural world. It's one of the most wrenching and honest accounts of falling in and out of love, of moving through a season of grief, that I've ever read."

—KAREN RUSSELL, author of *Swamplandia!*

TIM TARANTO

ARS BOTANICA

A Field Guide to Loss

CURBSIDE SPLENDOR

CURBSIDE SPLENDOR

Published by Curbside Splendor Publishing, Inc., Chicago, Illinois in 2017.

First Edition
Copyright © 2017 by Tim Taranto
Library of Congress Control Number: 2016961012
ISBN 978-1-940430-98-0

Edited by Naomi Huffman
Cover and interior design by Alban Fischer
Interior illustrations and author portrait by Tim Taranto
Cover botanical images © olga250/AdobeStock

Manufactured in the United States of America.

curbsidesplendor.com

For J

"Ineffectual certainly as memory is, but also transfigured as memory is."
—SØREN KIERKEGAARD

"You've been indexed
& written in pencil on bedroom walls
& like Shelley, writ in light
in a mind the size of a coin
conceived as memory
the beginning of sorrows"
—ELIZABETH WILLIS

"Orpheus hesitated beside the black river
With so much to look forward to he looked back.
We think he sang then, but the song is lost.
At least he had seen once more the beloved back
I say the song went this way: O prolong
Now the sorrow if that is all there is to prolong."
—DONALD JUSTICE

"So if my words don't come together, listen to the
melody 'cause my love's in there hiding."
—LEON RUSSELL

Dear Catalpa,

It's twelve below out and there are dead flowers on the table. Two fingers of gray water sit stagnant in the vase. I should compost the withered blossoms, but they are the chrysanthemums from her birthday party, and the others are mi meng hua, autumn lilacs that bloomed the night before Halloween, half-buried in a snow mound in a parking lot. A shrine of little curios — flowers, fossils, feathers — has been accumulating on this table, like the ad hoc memorials that form at the sites of car wrecks, or the "ghost bikes," painted white, you find chained to poles at intersections.

I started a painting again; it's an ink wash of a trilobite from my little table shrine. Contemplating the fossil, I thought, "this four hundred-million-year-old rock is not the trilobite, not the organism that scurried over the silty basement of a Devonian sea." This is not you, it is not her, it is nothing that happened to us. A painting of a fossil is not an actual fossil, the imprint of something lost and hardened with time. Still, I'm busying myself with this small, pains-taking rendering. Ink on paper.

What's the difference between living and thriving? Before I met her I was living. I was a composite of tastes and habits. I took fish oil, graded my papers in the sauna, played Magic, foraged in the woods, smoked a little pot, lit incense, and read in bed. And then your mother began leaving packages on my porch filled with food she'd prepared and slow dancing with me to Hank Williams on the radio. On walks, she'd unlace her fingers from mine and kneel to cut a white peony, lolling and crawling with ants on the Friends Meeting House lawn. By her side, I was a filled with a warm repose, how a houseplant must feel when moved to a sunny sill. I wrote on a scrap of something, almost automatically, after she'd left from visiting me at work: "sound of bell / calling me home." It was only for a short while, but reflected through her eyes, I started to feel beautiful for the first time in my life. There is this photo she texted me; in it, I'm naked and dreaming in her bed.

What's the difference between survival and good health? Considering the circumstances, what sort of life could we have expected for you? When she communicated her desire to terminate the pregnancy, I was with her, it was what I wanted, too. When she communicated her desire to terminate the relationship, I pulled my hat over my eyes and sank into her sofa. Maybe like seeing the world on the morning after you died, I was part of a new reality I could not imagine belonging to; I was afraid to move. What a prolonged and suffocating end to a luminous thing.

When I rose from the sofa, she said, "I don't know, I thought you'd argue."

"What for?" I said. I hated the sound of my voice, it hung in the air smug and helpless.

Her face was rinsed in amber, lit by the tea-lights on the table. She drew her hands to her mouth, as if she might blow into them to warm them. I cared for her as much that night as I do this freezing morning.

"I'm going to miss you," I said. And then, "Actually, I've missed you for such a long time."

She said, "I know you have."

I don't know why I'm wasting my time writing you, but I can't seem to do anything else. My students' work is piling up, ungraded, and I've got deadlines for the paper looming. I still owe them illustrations, and roughs were due last week for my column. One of my TAs has been covering my class.

What is happening? Is this the sound of a needle touching down on vinyl that is ringing through me, or the quietude of side B spinning to an end? To pursue this haunting, permit my light to shine through these pages so I might reach you through the darkness. I'll never draw with you. I won't pick wildflowers or scour the river's sandbars for geodes with you. I can't train your ear to recognize a tanager by its song. But I'll draw for you, create for you an ars botanica depicting a world you never knew. I'll tell you a story, too. I'll write you because loss does not end our relationships with the departed, it transforms them.

Queen Anne's Lace

(DAUCUS CAROTA)

At the center of each compound umbel is a single dark purple blossom — this is the "queen's blood." That almost black flower amid the rosette of white ones is what distinguishes the wild carrot, Queen Anne's lace.

ONE

"In Iowa, in the tall grass, there's a couple . . ."
—ARTHUR RUSSELL

LL I SEE IS DEATH," she said.

She gazed out over row crops, soybeans, and field after field of genetically modified corn. The morning rains were over and the overcast sky was glossed like the inside of an oyster shell. Wet corn stalks shivered in the silver light. The landscape bulged and curled, an earthen sea. A lone barn wore a fresh coat of white paint, skeletal windpumps turned exhaustedly in a nearly imperceptible wind. Herds of soot-colored clouds ebbed, then fled. It was a Marvin Cone painting. The world exhaled a worked and loamy breath.

"Iowa is beautiful," I said. "I heard someone say once how it possessed a subtle beauty, something about the oceanic skies. I never could see it, but now, my God."

An oriole, orange-breasted and onyx-winged, broke out in a solo from its perch on the powerline. Its song was trill and aqueous, more like a toy bird water whistle than a real bird.

"There's so many birds — oriole, osprey, killdeer — that from now on, whenever I see them, I'll think of you," she said.

As we biked on she switched into a lower gear and her derailleur made a rickety popping sound. The road bike was new to her, she was still getting the hang of it. We both had Bianchis, which she thought was cute, like our bikes were dating, too. She was an intrepid cyclist, racing down hills and powering up others like a nike. She once biked from the Oregon coast, through Yellowstone, across the continental divide, and back to Iowa on a solo tour. When my buddies back in Brooklyn asked to see a picture, I showed them the one of her triumphant by her bike at Hoosier Pass.

We wound down a series of wet country roads, nearing the raptor rehabilitation center at the lake's edge. The university funded the center for injured birds — hawks with talons mangled by traps, eagles full of lead shot pecked from deer carcasses, one-eyed owls and falcons peeled from the grills of pickups. These birds wouldn't make it in the wild. At dusk, Cypress, the old grandmother of a barred owl, answered calls from the free owls of the surrounding woods.

My ex used to volunteer at this raptor center, and I'd accompany her on the evening feedings. The freezers were stacked with bagged mice and rats, quail and pig fetuses, leftovers from the school of veterinary medicine. One of the volunteers told me the eagles loved fish when they could get it. That happened to be the summer I fished the Coralville dam daily, angling for walleye, but always incidentally hooking the unlucky carp. Carp are a handsome, muscular, and golden-scaled fish, but invasive, too, and it's illegal to throw them back. Some said the old Czech folks baked the carp at Christmastime, or that they were good for smoking, while most said they wouldn't eat carp for money. More often I was told carp made an excellent fertilizer for the pumpkin patch. But the carp I caught were a delicacy for the raptor center's eagles. The morning after I'd delivered a particularly hefty carp to Dolly, a thirty-year-old blind golden eagle, the volunteers discovered her preening on her perch, with the carp in one claw, and a decapitated raccoon — who had attempted to steal her fish — in the other.

"I love that. You should write that story," she said.

We biked side by side through the open gate of the raptor center. I scanned the woods. Our last time here, we cut boughs of blooming fragrant olive; their perfume filled her car for a week. But on this day we only noticed a few obscure white blossoms daubing the underbrush. And something bright orange and conflagrant: a chicken-of-the-woods mushroom, exploding up the trunk of a rotting oak. There must've been ten pounds of mushrooms, easy, but there was poison ivy everywhere, and we were in shorts.

"We'll be back for them," she said.

"We have to," I said.

She pedaled past me and rocketed down the hill. The terrain was steep, with the road flexing into a right angled curve at its base. Beyond the bend was a sparse patch of woods, beyond that the palisades, the lake below. She reached the corner as a black van appeared from the opposite direction. It was going to hit her.

I screamed her name. She braked. Her bike fishtailed on the wet road. The van swerved. They nearly collided. She vanished off the road and into the woods.

The van pulled over with its hazards flashing at the bottom of the hill. Her bike was in the ditch, but I didn't see her. I heard the tick-ticking of her rear wheel, turning with the momentum from the crash. I waded into the overgrown embankment and spotted something white crumpled at the foot of an oak. It was her shirt, and the rest of her. She was folded over, limp, with her arms out, like she was in child's pose.

"Please move," I said. "Please God, make her move, please."

She groaned and whimpered, pushing herself to her knees. "Babe," she said. "Help me get my shirt off."

Her face was bloody and stuck with debris. She tugged at the hem of her shirt. "I can't move my arm," she said.

"Your collarbone's broken," I said.

The bone buckled and swelled up red beneath her throat.

"No, it's not," she said.

I led her slowly by the hand up to the road where the driver of the van was shaking and saying, "Jesus, Jesus." He explained that he had to drop the kids off, but promised to return to give us a ride to the hospital. The van was full of elementary school kids on a field trip. I took his number, then he was gone, and we were alone.

I peeled my shirt off and offered it to her so she could clean her face. She asked if I could find her cigarettes, buried in her bag. I shook one out and planted it between her lips. There were scrapes across her forehead and brow, the bridge of her nose and chin. The twigs and leaves in her hair give her the look of a dryad, Daphne caught mid-transformation.

"What are you smiling about," she said, and smiled.

"Nothing, it's stupid."

"You don't smoke," she said.

"Nope, never once," I said, and lit my cigarette, then hers.

"Don't. Please, babe."

"Now seems like the right time, doesn't it?" I didn't inhale, just puffed a little, rolling the smoke in my mouth like a cigar.

"You were crying," she said.

"No I wasn't."

"You were when you found me, I saw."

Some park workers showed up in a golf cart, followed finally by the park director in her truck. She ordered the park workers around and radioed for an ambulance. She fashioned a sling out of her raincoat.

Later, police and state troopers, firefighters, EMTs, and ambulance drivers all asked the same questions. "How old are you?"

"Twenty-six," she said.

"Are you taking any medication?" they asked.

"Antidepressants," she repeated, over and over.

A shy bald cop leaned in and said, "Me too, couldn't live without them."

They all asked if she was wearing a helmet, and she kept saying, "No, no."

They wheeled her on a stretcher to the rear of the ambulance, and she wiggled the hand of her free arm into a wave. She asked the EMTs if I could ride in the ambulance with her, but they said no.

She mouthed the words, "I hate this," as they shut her in the ambulance, and I mouthed back, "I know." And then, even though we'd only been dating two months, "I love you."

A state trooper around my age, a combat veteran and father of three, gave me a lift to the ER.

"I don't believe in any God," he said, "but I'll credit Lady Luck. She was looking out for your wife."

"Girlfriend," I said.

"I responded to a call last week," he said. "Similar deal: female cyclist, one vehicle, and heck, brother, they just cremated her. I don't know where they scattered her ashes, but I think it was Lake McBride. I bet you could Google the obit and find out."

I was sitting with her best friend, Ingrid, in the ER when the young nurse carted her in.

"My collarbone is broken. The impact shattered my shoulder blade," she said. "They took a million x-rays, and they kept asking me if I was pregnant."

"God, no, that would be the absolute worst," said Ingrid.

"I know," she said.

I didn't know it, Ingrid didn't know it, and she didn't know it for certain, but as her feet unclipped from the pedals, as she flew through the air like a meteor, as she collided with that tree, as her bones broke and her blood gushed from her body, as bruises bloomed on her skin, she was already three weeks pregnant.

Mi Meng Hua

(BUDDLEJA DAVIDII)

This ornamental flowering shrub is native to Asia and common in the US. We called it by their Chinese name, mi meng hua, but it is also referred to as butterfly bush and autumn lilac. When I met her, she candied lilacs. When I dream her, she's candying lilacs.

Dear Catalpa,

You would've had tattooed parents. While I inspected my first tattoo, irritated and oozing under the plastic wrap, I thought: if I have a kid, they'll only know me this way, these drawings on my skin will be as familiar to them as the summer constellations.

An early memory of mine — possibly my first — is a memory of a tattoo. I'm riding on the shoulders of my father, your would-be grandfather, as we pass through the dim halls of the Mystic Aquarium in Connecticut. The saltwater tanks glow with a jade light that reflects in my father's glasses. There are squadrons of barracuda, ghostly rays, a snaggletoothed shark, a living fossil.

I ask, "What are those?" pointing at its gills.

"Those lines? Tattoos," says my father. "That's how you know he's a daddy shark."

He set me down and rolled up his sleeve, exposing his blue-green anchor, his eagle with its wings spread over his bicep, my mother's name in faded script. "All dads get tattoos," he said.

Had you been born, your mother would've held you in tattooed arms. Hers are a mix of professional work and stick-and-poke jobs, illustrations and glyphs owing to different times, marking different events in her life, her friends, her travels. I suppose one could draw inferences from these inked scars the way a dendrochronologist reads the stories in the cross sections of trees. As a birder, though, I can't ignore her bird tattoos. She has two: a crow and an owl. Your paternal grandmother's maiden name is Crow.

The barn owl on her bicep in particular struck me. Lorine Niedecker contemplated the owl, *What / is it the sign / of? The sign of / an owl.* Which may be enough for Lorine, but in my life owls have always served as spiritual wayfinders, marked the presence of the supernatural. Owls were my grandmother's familiar, and whenever I see one, the living bird or their representation, I feel her. Just before she passed away, she came to live with us in the Catskills. Her room was populated with owls: stitched into pillows and reproduced on postcards, figurines roosting on the mantle, stained glass owls gleaning sun in her window. She kept a music box on her desk, topped with a barn owl statuette that, when wound, played "Sunrise

Sunset" from *Fiddler on the Roof*. I'd hide under the dining room table with the owl music box in my lap, listening until the tune stumbled to a stop, and then I'd wind it up and listen all over again.

The day we met, I was having dinner with my best friend Ed, and she was working the bar, and maybe it's cheesy to say so, but she felt significant to me even then, like I was seeing a good friend from my past after many years. When she raised her arm to pluck a pen from her hair, I saw her owl.

Ed was watching me watch her. "Not your type," he said.

"Then I guess you've never really known me," I said.

"Nobody knows you better," he said.

We were in Iowa; I knew I'd see her again.

She has another tattoo I forgot until recently, a self-inflicted ankh, "the breath of life," washing out on her ankle. These days I find myself imagining it to be imbued with mystical healing powers, a ward against suffering, a poultice for any misfortune that should befall her, and in this way, the hieroglyph has given me some peace in her absence. Even if she doesn't believe it, I hang on to the hope that some god is keeping watch over her. Maybe the light's been left on in the kitchen, or the back door is unlocked for her. Maybe that god is with her now, in this ten-degree night that "feels like negative fourteen." I dream that some little god, ankh in hand, is with her at the end of each day to ease her weariness. And there, too when an Everly Brothers song comes on the radio to share in her joy. Listen to me! Somehow, you've made your father into a believer again, or a psychotic.

I had breakfast with Rabbi Gold today. I was kind of a mess. He put his hand on my shoulder and told me every child leaves a mark on their parent.

"I'm not a parent, I never was," I said. "I just miss her."

"Okay," he said. "But hear me out. For some fathers, a mark isn't made until their kid is old enough to toss a football or practice the cello. Your child has made a mark on you while still in the womb, without ever being born. What a gift you have to feel so deeply, and what a burden, too."

I guess in a way he's right, because a month after you were gone, I had a trilobite tattooed on my arm. In the sky somewhere between Des Moines and Phoenix, a freckled stewardess asked about it.

"It looks like a teeny tiny coffin," she said.

"A sarcophagus." I said.

"Exactly! For a baby mummy," she said, and giggled.

I said, "You nailed it. That's what it is."

Trilobite

(TRILOBITA)

These marine arthropods ruled the paleozoic seas up until the Permian extinction. Their fossils turn up in Iowa's riverbeds and in the hills of New York. Finding them out here makes me feel a little less homesick. The last picture she sent me was one of her holding a trilobite fossil.

TWO

"That only God, my dear, / Could love you for yourself alone, /
And not your yellow hair."

—W.B. YEATS

HE CLUNG TO TO ME, soaking my shirt as I lifted her from the bath. I toweled her off, held her as she stepped into her panties, pulled them down for her so she could pee. We hadn't really left the house since she was discharged from the hospital.

We ordered in for pizza again and ate on the back porch. Her painkillers started to kick in, her sentences were slow and slurred.

"He's a great human being, amazing, but it just came down to the fact that he lived a pretty comfortable life," she said. "And I'm privileged. You are, too. I'm not saying you have to be orphaned or homeless, but you need to experience at least one non-lethal death in your life. To have any sort of significant—" she hummed in pursuit of the right word, "—perspective, I guess? Do you know what I mean?"

"I do. I could say the same for my ex," I said.

"Is this scary?" she asked.

"Is what scary?"

"What we're doing, you and me," she said. "I told my family to get used to you, that you're not going anywhere."

"I ain't goin' nowhere."

"Where did you come from?" She asked. She kissed my ear.

"You know, you wouldn't have liked me back when I had hair."

"I've seen pictures. I creeped on you on Facebook when we first met," she said. She tore at her pizza with her fingers, balled up some excess cheese, tossed it into the hostas.

"I was such a piece of shit, though," I said. "Like a cartoon of a preppy, Brooklyn cocksucker."

"Hush," she said. "Eat my crust."

I'll begin after it ended, at Zeus's birthday party at that Senegalese restaurant in Fort Greene. A blizzard hit the city, closed the schools and bridges, turned the streets into tunnels, transformed cars into white effigies. I was using my finger to draw in the condensation on the cold window that looked out onto the street while everybody at my table shouted and laughed. An old college friend visiting from Los

Angeles touched my arm and introduced herself, asked how I knew Zeus. Confusion, recognition, and then embarrassment ran over her face as she began to remember that we'd actually known each other since undergrad. Perhaps she recalled how we'd hooked up one night, years ago. She pretended as if she'd known it was me all along, that she was only playing a joke. For her sake, I went along with it.

"How are *you*?" she said, and took my hand in a way she intended to seem sympathetic or earnest.

Considering the transformation that had occurred in my body, I couldn't blame her. In car mirrors and in the storefront windows along Court Street, in the bathroom mirror in the teacher's lounge, and in the photos from my cousin's wedding, I barely recognized myself.

"Well," I said, "I don't have cancer or anything, if that's what you're thinking."

Back at the end of June, during the Montauk Century Ride, I reclined in the grass beside a man who looked a bit like Larry David. He was stretched out with his eyes closed, he gnawed a wedge of melon. "The only way to survive New York is to get the fuck out of Dodge any chance you can. Otherwise you'll end up blowing your brains out the back of your head." He wasn't talking to me — I don't know who he was talking to — but I heeded this oracle with devotion and doubt in equal measures. At the start of the July Fourth weekend, I boarded the Metro North for New Haven to meet Sun. From there we headed up to Deerfield for Ed's twenty-fifth birthday.

Ed, the birthday boy, greeted us in the driveway, sweaty from a run in the woods. He filled some juice jars with a mead he'd brewed with his dad, and I carried mine into the bathroom with me and changed into my trunks. I chugged the mead, refilled the jar halfway with an Islay from my flask, chugged that, then brushed my teeth. Outside the little bathroom window, cottonball clouds moseyed over a pasture of blue heaven, red-winged blackbirds and bobolinks sounded off from the fence of the neighbor's dairy farm, Ed's chocolate labs sparred on the lawn. I was already feeling drunk. I told myself, *I could live here.*

A quick drive through a circuit of maple-lined roads brought us to a falls and swimming hole. Families picnicked on the rocks and teenagers leapt, shrieking and splashing into the gorge. The soil there, exposed in the cliffs, was folded with clots of gray clay. People dredged it over their skin, allowing the paste to cake and crumble on their faces and chests.

I applied the clay like war paint, worked it into my beard and smeared it through my hair. Then I tried napping on the rocks while Sun and Ed swam, but I was jolted awake with a sensation that I was falling through the ground. Even in the county, I was a clenched fist.

"The sun, a ripe persimmon, nests in the black branches," I said to myself. "And it can't help me." I waded into the chill limestone pool until the water swallowed me up to my throat. I dunked my head and rinsed out the clay. Toweling off near the car, I found a bald patch, the size of a cockleshell, located on my scalp just north of my left ear.

"Looks like alopecia areata," Ed's father, a physician, said later that day. "It's not anything to worry about, health-wise. But keep an eye on it."

It wasn't the first unexplained occurrence of hair loss I'd experienced. When Ian died in a house fire sophomore year, my hair washed out in the shower, whole clumps of it collecting in the drain. During my first year in New York, when I was unemployed and crashing at my sister Ruth's, calling in to WNYC as an unsolicited fact checker, pacing the apartment naked with a joint, I'd slept with my yoga instructor and she'd given me scabies. My hands itched all day, and my stomach itched after the shower, though everything itched worse in bed. I got a prescription for a pesticide cream and was instructed to apply it over my whole body. The lashes on the lower lid of my left eye curled wildly and fell out not long after that. I figured it was due to the cream; I didn't think much of it at the time.

As soon as I got back from Western Mass, I got an appointment with a dermatologist who was heralded as the best. Already, the bald spot had doubled in size, and two smaller patches had appeared over the opposite ear. In the examination room, I nervously rubbed one of the new bald spots until the doctor entered. He was so tan and his teeth were so white they seemed to glow. His hairline was so low, his scalp so replete with hair, that I knew there was no way this man could understand how I felt. It didn't take long before he echoed Ed's father's diagnosis: I had alopecia, but at that stage it was difficult to determine which type. If it was areata, an autoimmune disease that produces bald patches and brittle fingernails, the effects could be reversed with treatment. If it was an early stage of a more vicious variety of alopecia — totalis or universalis, in which the body purges itself of all keratin cells, hair, and nails, even the microscopic cilia in the nose and ears — then there would be little hope for regrowth.

There was a chance I'd be hairless for the rest of my life.

"Not likely," said my doctor. "But I'm going to zap these locations today, and we'll see where we're at in a few weeks." He jabbed a needle into my scalp a dozen or so times.

"Some people say this hurts, but I know you can take it. You're a tough guy," he said.

It hurt. A lot. He wrote me a prescription for a topical cream, and his assistant wrote me a reminder for a follow-up.

My anxiety wouldn't let me sleep. If I managed to drift off, I'd wake with visions of bedbugs crawling in my sheets. The best I could do was go to the roof with the French press in hand and wait for dawn. In the morning cold, I eavesdropped on the grackles chattering, mimicking car alarms, cell phone chimes, sirens. Once, while my roommates were still asleep, I left a poem on the dry-erase board that included a line about the grackles, and other things that I felt were harbingers of our planet's demise. When I got home from work, someone had titled my poem "GRACK

KILLS," and added an illustration of a penis cactus wearing a sombrero.

The steroids worked, sort of. They pushed up archipelagos of dark, pube-like hairs. But they were short lived; they vanished as rapidly as they emerged.

"When did you start shaving your arms?" Lily asked.

"I didn't shave them," I said.

"Weird, I never noticed."

My friend Lily and I walked through a colonnade of dapple-trunked London Planes in Maria Hernandez Park, sipping horchata. A group of teenagers were eating sour Skittles, drinking Big Cans, and laughing loudly on a stoop. A young woman was cornrowing a young boy's hair; a friend teased them and threw a Skittle in their direction.

Lily tickled my forearm. "Well, I really wish I had your hairless arms!" she said. "Would you judge me if I got electrolysis? Not everywhere, just like my ape arms and my 'stache."

"It's your body," I said.

I started spending my sleepless nights on the internet. I'd untag myself from group pictures, like the one taken at a picnic on Governor's Island, another my sister Ruth had posted of our family at the Gauguin show at the Corcoran. In it, I looked like a fugitive, with my hat pulled down over my ears, my fleece zipped over my mouth. Ed emailed a photo of me, Sun, and Zeus at the Blaschka glass exhibit. I had a little ponytail in that picture, a beard, too, and looking at the picture made me cry. I ordered a new pair of glasses online with rims thick enough to mask my thinning eyebrows. I Googled wigs and WedMD-ed autoimmune diseases, and everything I discovered made me feel a little more hopeless.

Packages arrived weekly from my mother. She sent biotin and shark cartilage supplements, incense and extracts, shampoos and tinctures, but it was all snake oil. My pubes were gone, and exactly half my scalp was bald. To make her feel better, I told her I'd noticed some regrowth since I started applying the tea tree oil to the affected areas, and that my nails felt stronger after a week of the folic acid.

"Shit, you've gotten faster!" said Johanna. She was stretching, her foot hooked on a bench at Grand Army Plaza.

I'd been running in Prospect Park in the mornings before work, and then again when I got home. "I'm just trying to regain some control over my body," I said.

"That fucking dog, though," she said.

A shepherd mix had chased me on the trail near the boathouse, barking furiously. I'd always been great with dogs, but now I was driving them mad. Babies, too. Babies used to adore me, now I made them bawl.

"I think it's my hair, or lack thereof," I said.

"You're invisible?" she said, reaching for her toes.

"Yeah, like they can't smell me," I said. "Hair traps smells, and dogs communicate through scent. All mammals do, to some extent."

"Could be fear they're sensing," she said.

"I'm like this big hairless mammal they can't identify. It freaks them out," I said.

"Or it's just your fear," she said.

My fingernails didn't fall off in the way I imagined, popping off like pistachio shells. Instead, they withered, flaked, and eventually peeled off in bloody strands, exposing my raw cuticles. Without fingernails, I couldn't even pick up a heads-up nickel or unlace my sneakers. Buttoning my pants was a struggle. In a Korean nail salon on Smith Street, I waited to have a full set of acrylics put on. Gluing fake nails to my nailbeds was Lily's suggestion, and it beat the alternative: blood-soaked Band-Aids bound around each fingertip. The technician was polite and smelled like fruit juice.

"You think you're weird, I can tell, but you're not weird," she said.

"I don't think I'm weird," I said.

"Many Brooklyn men now come for the manicure and pedicure," she said. "You're not weird at all."

At a house concert on the Upper West Side, a neighbor of the host asked why I was wearing a knit hat indoors when it was August, and everyone else was shvitzing. He yanked off my cap and guffawed.

"Holy shit! You look like a penis!" he said.

"I'm sick," I said.

He put a hand to his mouth and apologized. "Chemo?"

"No, nothing like that," I said. "It's autoimmune."

"Oh, thank God. You're a lucky son-of-a-bitch."

I fumbled through the little I knew about my condition, and he told me alopecia wasn't a big deal. He told me it was a gift.

"Do you know how many of my friends would have killed to have had what you've got?" he said. "Do you know what they went through to shave their bodies?" He made a comical gesture to his dick and balls. "Shit, they drove the boys wild! Down in the Village, they'd pull off their wigs and they'd be practically jerking off on their bald heads! That was New York in the eighties though, and those boys are all gone now."

Upon seeing me for the first time after summer break, a fellow teacher at the Montessori school was curious about the bet I'd lost. A second-grade student told me she liked me better when I had eyebrows. I told her I liked me better then, too. The horrified homeroom teacher apologized to me, and coerced the kid into an apology she neither meant nor comprehended. My principal said she was sympathetic to everything I was going through, but the school had a dress code that extended to the faculty, and she'd prefer it if I didn't wear my hat in the classroom.

"I want you to know that I've done some research about your situation," she said, twirling her finger in a halo around her blonde curls.

"I've read it's genetic, but nobody in my family . . ." I said.

"Well, I read that the triggers are mental," she said. "I'm asking you to take care of yourself. Do you understand what I'm trying to say to you?"

The school psychologist placed me in touch with a therapist in Park Slope. During our first session he explained that he felt my hair loss was in response to stress.

"Do you know what I'm looking at right now?" the therapist asked me. "I'm looking at an attractive man sitting in my office, and a smart man. I don't see a bald man sitting here."

We agreed to meet at the same time in two weeks, but I never went back.

I visited my brother Lyman at the bar where he worked and handed him a Pyrex container of chard enchiladas.

"It's better warm," I said.

"I'm going to attack this now," he said. He ordered me a rye.

"Someone told me I looked like the Zig-Zag tobacco guy tonight," he said. He twisted the ends of his mustache and held his phone up to his face. On the screen was the image of the Zig-Zag logo. "The Zig-Zag dude, you know?"

The bartender slid me the drink, and I handed it to my brother. "I'm taking a break," I said.

He patted my shoulder. "You had a way better beard, buddy," he said. "Sorry."

"There's nothing to apologize about," I said.

One of the regulars, a cabbie, asked if I was the bald brother. He removed his hat and glasses, and I saw that he, too, had alopecia. His scalp looked pink and wrinkled and gross. There were fleshy pads where his eyebrows once were, his eyelids appeared red and chapped. Seeing other people with alopecia made me anxious and sick to my stomach. Once, on an Amtrak train, I spotted a woman with alopecia and switched cars to get away from her.

The only thing the cabbie wanted to talk about as he drove me home was our shared disease. He showed me pictures from the different alopecia conferences he'd attended in St. Louis and Seattle, photos of him posing beside his hairless comrades, rubbing each other's bald heads. He wanted to fix me up with a nice bald girl he knew that lived in Sheepshead Bay.

"Don't worry," he said. "She wears a wig."

Before leaving his cab, I promised I'd join him at the next alopecia support group meeting at Weill. I asked him how much the fare was, but he refused to let me pay.

"We stick together, brother," he said.

I told him I'd see him at the meeting, no matter what.

My father was taking the Amtrak up from DC. the following morning. I woke up early with the apartment still dark and bumped along the walls to the bathroom. I winced in the bright light over the sink and was astonished by what I saw in the mirror. I ran my fingers over my cheeks and scalp, examining my reflection from all angles. There was a delicate stubble, a dusting of hair on my head and chin — eyebrows, lashes, hair everywhere.

Nope — not a miracle. It was just another healing dream, a desperate wishing dream. I woke up feeling like I'd just lost all over again what had already been taken from me.

I was late meeting my father and Lyman at McSorley's. I ordered a round of two-and-twos for the table, threw each of my mugs back down in a single go, and ordered another round.

"I thought you were taking a break," Lyman said.

"I didn't say that," I said.

"You feeling alright?" my father asked.

"I'm fine," I said. "Seriously."

My father and brother exchanged a look.

"I saw that, I'm not blind. I said I'm fine, I'm *fine*."

"Okay, no one here thinks otherwise," said my father. He picked up the tab, and we headed to Chelsea. There were some

Richard Serra prints my father wanted to see. While waiting to cross Broadway, I took in my brother with his wooly beard and tar-black top-knot, my father with his snow-capped scalp and white beard that got whiter each year, like the muzzle of an old dog.

"I want to duck into Harry's first," said my father.

My father's buddy Harry had a print shop near the gallery. Looking at the shop — once a corner grocery — there were twin lithos, a diptych of wild irises, one in each window. I'd been meaning to visit him since I moved to New York, but hadn't managed to make it work. The door chimed as we entered. The place reeked of the familiar odor of ink and cigars and thinners. Harry still wore overalls and his glasses on a cord around his neck, which he placed on his nose when he saw us enter. He rose from his drafting table and gripped my father by the shoulders. Dark ink illuminated the fibrous cracks of his fingers and knuckles.

"Holy Moses, Paul," said Harry, looking at me, and then Lyman. "I don't have to guess which one of these mooks is your son!" said Harry.

Lyman put his arm around my shoulders. I used to be the one that looked more like dad.

On the way to my doctor's appointment, I felt like everyone on the G train was staring at me because of my alopecia. Or maybe they were staring because I was wearing a hooded fleece and a Carhartt beanie on a ninety-eight degree day. And what was I hiding? A copse of hairs on my skull that I was still reluctant to shave. I guess it felt too much like a surrender.

The orange-skinned doctor sauntered in with one hand in the pocket of his white coat, the other thumbing with his phone. "Hold up, Jed," he said.

I didn't bother to correct him. Examining my feet dangling from the examining table, I noticed the hairs that once curled from the knuckles of my big toes were all gone.

"You're going to love this," he said. "My wife wanted me to show you this." He nose-laughed. "Take a look at this," he said, and handed me his phone.

"Vin Diesel?" I said.

"Bingo!" he said. "There's more, scroll down. Bruce Willis, Jason Statham, Yul Brynner. Patrick Stewart."

"Captain Jean-Luc Picard," I said.

"You know what these men have in common?" he said. "They're sex symbols, every one." He jabbed a finger at my head. "*This*, a bald head, is in. It's what women want nowadays. Trust me, women get wet for bald dudes! I wish I was bald! Be glad this isn't the seventies. Be thankful you're not a woman with alopecia."

He told me he was ending my treatment; I had universalis after all, and regrowth, for me, was pretty much out of the question.

Ruth rented a car for Labor Day weekend and Lyman and I drove with her through the Catskills to our childhood home which, since our parents' move to DC, had become our family's country house. The well-worn experience of this drive, the same rivers and mountains and trees passing by the windows like a zoetrope, felt distinctly changed this time. Everything had taken on the proportions of a memory-dream. At the Delaware Water Gap, I spotted an osprey soaring over the river, and I imagined my body below, floating up the Susquehanna against the current.

We got dinner at the landmark Italian restaurant in our hometown. While Ruth and Lyman were outside smoking, I stayed in the booth drawing flowers and fossils on my placemat. A waitress came over.

"Why do I feel like I know you?" she asked.

I knew exactly who she was — my childhood crush. I'd recognized her as soon as I had entered the restaurant and spotted her laughing beside the oven with one of the cooks.

"I've just got one of those faces," I said.

"I think you're pulling my leg," she said. "You're related to the Piedmonts that live in that big white house on the park."

"I am. I'm their cousin," I said.

"I knew it!" she said. A thin wedding band glinted on her finger. She wore it as naturally as a childhood scar.

"Tell Ted Piedmont Claire says hi," she said.

The three of us walked home, crossing the green steel trestle, passing the firehouse, the clock tower, old Groton Academy, the Revolutionary War monument, the Masonic temple. The bats came out and celebrated the arrival of night with an aerial show, darting in erratic patterns over our driveway.

I packed my one-hitter and toked it alone behind the carriage barn. The boughs of the towering Norwegian spruces swayed with an almost maternal care and the whole Milky Way spilled out above. I exhaled a lungful of Catskill air, and declared that this whole thing had been out of my control since it began. I confessed this to the brown bats, the pines and the lilac bushes, the river, the stars, the entire summer night, to myself. As if to voice her affirmation, a great-horned owl clucked and hooted overhead in the eaves of the barn.

There were too many lights on in the house. Our parents' records were scattered on the oriental rug in the formal dining room. Ruth and Lyman were sifting through boxes of photos in the kitchen.

"Will you shave me?" I asked Ruth.

Upstairs in the hall, Lyman found the clippers that our mother used to shave our heads with each summer on the night before swim lessons. There wasn't much hair to buzz — it fell on my shoulders and fluttered into the sink like soft asterisms of down. Lyman asked if I wanted to save the clippings, and I told him no, thank you. There weren't any hairs to raise on my arms or on the back of my neck, but still little bumps appeared as soon as my sister applied the cold shave gel to my head. Ruth steered her pink razor carefully over the contours of my skull. She handed me the razor, and asked if I wanted to shave my own chin and lip, my cheeks and jaw, my lone eyebrow, for what would be the last time in my life.

I never really talked about the alopecia stuff until I told it all to her. She encouraged me to write about it, too, and I finally did. I read the story to an auditorium full of high school students at a summer writing camp in town. She was seated in the back, smiling at me, her sling strapped under her shawl; I was reading only to her.

It was the strangest thing, but after I met her, for the first time in five years, hair started sprouting ecstatically from my knees and face.

Norwegian Spruce

(PICEA ABIES)

"Can I pluck it?"

"I don't care."

"Don't you think this is crazy? What if all your hair is coming back?"

"It wouldn't matter one way or the other."

"Whoa! It's so long. You're growing a mustache. What do you think this means?"

"It's the effect you have on my body."

"Oh, stop."

Dear Catalpa,

What else should you know about me? My older sister, your aunt Ruth, lives in Brooklyn, as does your uncle, my kid brother Lyman. I love black licorice. I can't whistle. I'm a connoisseur of liniments and medicated balms. I can sleep almost anywhere, under any conditions. I've snored on the couch through raging house parties and dozed supine on the carpet of the Cedar Rapids airport. I'm completely hairless, but you know that. Also, I'm something of a limbo king.

No matter the state of my body (I've battled with obesity most of my life), I've always been something of a wonder when it comes to the limbo. I'm a fine yogi, and a seasoned distance runner, but I have a hunch the source of my limbo powers are more than physiological, owing instead to some supernatural enchantment, which I hope, for your case, is hereditary. Display your limbo skill with modesty, kid. Reserve it for moments of utter necessity (also luaus and bar mitzvahs).

Years before I met your mother, I was at a rooftop party in the

West Village. It was a party for a sculptor who'd attended Saint Ann's with the woman I was dating at the time. I'd hung out with the hostess on several occasions, and my date admired her, though I always got an aloof, too-cool vibe from her. We showed up early, and I kept to myself until the party grew to a vibrant hum, made evident by the number of people dancing to Mariah Carey. It was about that time that someone whipped out the limbo stick.

"Hold my hat," I said to my date, and tossed her my beanie.

I didn't play my hand too cool. While folks were stumbling to the stick, pelvis first, only to fall on their asses with their hands groping at the air, I was limboing with the speed and agility of a lizard racing over hot sand, whole hand-lengths of clearance between my body and the limbo stick. Soon, everyone on the roof was watching. In the end, it was down to me and an Israeli modern dancer. Though she dueled with grit and honor, I left her in the dust of the battlefield for the wild dogs to gnaw and the scavenging birds to peck. I bowed to the cheers of the entire party, and even the hostess condescended to have her picture taken with me.

On the subway ride home I was exuberant and chatty in the manner of a victorious athlete in the locker room. It was several stops before I realized that my partner sat silent.

"Didn't think I could limbo?" I asked.

"It's not that," she said. "You weren't wearing your hat."

"I know. It would've fallen off," I said.

"I had to explain all night to people that you don't have cancer or something," she said. "Everyone wanted to know what's wrong with you. I don't mind talking about it, but it was just a lot for me, and I wasn't exactly ready for all that."

"I'm sorry," I said.

"Don't apologize," she said.

The train was being held at the station, train traffic ahead.

"Should I wear a wig?" I said.

"This isn't easy for me. Do you know that?" she said.

But anyone who has loved anybody, or loved anything really, knows loving is not always easy. That night on the G train, the two of us weren't really in love.

I was often hatless around your mother, or at least I was hatless around her more than anyone else, ever. She desired me, bald and overweight as I was — it's the only way she ever knew me. She loved me this way.

I love her: this person who I watched the stars from my roof with, who I watched nearly lose her life, who I cared for in the wake of her accident, who I stood by during the pregnancy and in the dark times after the abortion, this person who became my best friend. I love her: this person who, after all of it, left me behind. If I go outside tonight, alone, and there's an ice ring around this full moon — like every good thing I possibly see — I'll see it once for her, and another time for me.

Barred Owl

(STRIX VARIA)

Lacks ear tufts, large dark eyes, mottled brown "barred" plumage. Native to the eastern United States, but range has expanded to include the Midwest, Iowa. Caterwauling call sounds like, "Who cooks for you? Who cooks for you?"

"I want to cook for you."

"Yeah, cook what?"

"Anything. I'm learning how to make ostrich sausage. I've been candying lilacs."

Dear Catalpa,

If I'm to believe that through hoping or imagining you can read these letters, hear these stories, and look at these drawings, then if I played you a song, couldn't you hear it? The track I want to play for you is "Trap Queen" by Fetty Wap. It's not my favorite song, but it was our song in way.

Fetty (Willie Maxwell II) hails from Paterson, New Jersey, same as William Carlos Williams. Just as WCW penned his fair share of pop poems pertaining to plums and rain-glazed wheelbarrows, Fetty Wap proved himself to be a poet celebrity as well, most notably with his track "Trap Queen." For us, "Trap Queen" served like a repository for all of our halcyon memories from that first summer. We'd sing along in the car as Fetty crooned about getting high with his baby, going to the mall and riding with his baby, counting stacks with his baby. We'd sing loudest when he said he was in the kitchen cooking pies with his baby — your mother is an amazing baker. It was a radio jam, and a love song, we were into it, it was where we were.

Back then, we were pretty carefree. We got up at noon and biked around singing Paul Simon's *Rhythm of the Saints*, whipped up elaborate breakfasts, and craned our necks searching for shooting stars. We harvested nettles for soups and mushrooms for quiches, we explored the meadows and cemeteries sharing stories from our childhoods. We had "big plans" for a pizza date in the Grand Canyon. I don't think I wrote a single sentence of a story or a line of a poem that whole summer. It's a lousy truth, but I'm afraid good art doesn't get made when you're that blissed out.

At the height of the Blissed Out Era, I left her to to fly back east for my co-teacher's retirement party. In Brooklyn, my friends showed me new ramen spots and took me out on the boat to watch the sun set on the Hudson. I was really only going along to jot down recipe ideas, snap photos, and collect the choicest bits and dispatches to relay back to her.

"While the female osprey remains on the nest, the male spends weeks on the wing, scouring marshes for bluefish and buoys, pieces of rope, hula hoops, police tape, anything his mate desires," I said, in a David Attenborough voice to her on the phone. When I asked what she wanted from New York, she said, "Baby, just you." Still, I dragged a hungover Lyman with me into tea shop after tea shop all down Canal and into Brooklyn's 8th Avenue Chinatown, hunting for her favorite oolongs and pu-erhs. We made a detour to my old neighborhood to go to Four & Twenty Blackbirds, and waited in line for half an hour to buy their pie cookbook for her.

With the cookbook and tins of loose tea on my lap, I watched as Brooklyn surrendered to the marshed sprawl of the Rockaways on my way to JFK. I asked the cabbie to turn up the radio. I'd never heard the song that was playing before, somebody rapping about having a good time with his girlfriend — I could relate. I Googled the lyrics, it was "Trap Queen," and I brought that song back for her as well.

A huge storm roosted over most of the Mid Atlantic. Flights were delayed and canceled, rescheduled. After a full day trapped in a leaking LaGuardia terminal, I boarded the last and only flight out to Chicago. But in Chicago, all the planes were grounded for the night — I wouldn't be back in Iowa until morning. I stayed that night with one of my oldest friends Zeus at his loft in Wicker Park. All night your mother sent me selfies and photos of her baking vegan cookies. I sent her "Trap Queen," and she sent back a video that began with rain drumming her sunroof. She panned to the condensed windshield of her car. Her finger came into the frame, and slowly drew a cartouche containing two hearts on the glass. The last time I drove her car, the remnants of these two hearts were still smudged on the windshield.

I hear they've got a room in the Vatican where the bishops and cardinals weep with the new pontiff for the burden of his charge. The course I taught last semester, Creative Writing for the Musician, ended up looking a lot like that crying room in Rome.

"The good news is that for the next eighteen weeks, every one of you can be an artist," I said to my seventeen undergrads. It was early in the semester, they behaved like there was a carbon monoxide leak in the room, maybe two of them were taking notes. "The bad news, though," I said, "is that the unhewn ore of real artmaking is the intimate suffering of each and every one of you."

I wish one of them had, at that moment, interrupted me with a fart, ripped like a single note from a cornet. I wish one of them had produced a boombox from under their desk, pressed play, and bumped "Trap Queen" at a full volume, cueing the the whole class to break into a flashmob dance. Who was I kidding? They didn't need art the way I did, because they were all, as far as I could tell, pretty okay. They weren't a haunting like the human at the front of the room, the one that gathered his dry erase markers at the close of class and contemplated jumping into the path of a speeding car each time he crossed Dubuque. I certainly didn't need art to save my life during the Blissed Out Era; back then my life didn't need saving. I didn't have any use for God or philosophy or art, and why would I? You weren't a star on the horizon. And me? I was in the kitchen, cooking pies with your mother.

Poison Ivy

(TOXICODENDRON RADICANS)

Oil in the leaves causes the itch. One summer, Lyman and I got poison ivy, bad.

"We take navy showers in this house, isn't that right, sailors?" said our father. We laughed and shivered and scratched our bodies. "I know it itches something fierce, but you're Piedmonts, and Piedmonts never feel pain." He squirted Tecnu in our hands, then readied his stopwatch. "Ready, sailors?"

"I like that story," she said. "Is your brother still your best friend?"

"You're my best friend."

THREE

"Nursing her I felt alive / in the animal moment, / scenting the predator. / Her death was the worst thing / that could happen, / and caring for her was best."

—DONALD HALL

HAT IS IT?" I ASKED. As soon as she got in the car, she handed me grocery bag with something heavy and cold in it. With her injuries I did all the driving, and as a New Yorker with just an Iowa learner's permit, she was teaching me how to drive. I raised and lowered the bag, gauging the weight.

"Guess," she said.

"Hmm . . . a lamb's head?"

"Ding! Ding! Ding!"

I knew what it was, we'd been talking about roasting a lamb's head for some time. When we got home, I called my father and asked for his mother's recipe for Capozzelli di Angnelli.

On the counter, she attempted to roll out the dough for the quiche one-handed.

"Help!" she said.

She took over as executive chef, and I the sous. She deejayed on her phone, sipped wine, and read the recipes to me as I measured oregano into a teaspoon and packed the head with breadcrumbs, garlic, and oil-cured olives. Its black lips were peeled back, and the lamb looked like it was grinning at us from the Dutch oven. She doused it with some of the wine, and we covered it with a lid.

"You know this dish is total peasant's food," I said.

"We're peasants," she said.

With the lamb in the oven, we thought we'd try a short walk. We hadn't gone on a walk or anything like that since the accident.

"You can pull harder. It doesn't hurt," she said. I stood behind her, watching our reflection in the hall mirror as I struggled to put her hair in a ponytail.

"Good. Now wrap the elastic around one more time," she said. "Hey, not bad! You'll get there," she said. She turned her head, inspecting my work. It sucked, but she winked at me in the mirror anyways.

"Help!" she yelled from the doorway. I kneeled down to tie her shoes.

The road steamed from the day's rain — it had been a wet summer.

We walked slowly, arm in arm down the sidewalk. We stopped and cut Canada lilies growing wild in an overgrown yard. She plucked a real estate brochure from a signpost in that same yard.

"Look," she said. "Lamb's quarters!" She pointed out a whole patch of lamb's quarters sprouting beside a garage in the alley.

"It's a lamb-themed night."

"My mom says I'm lucky," she said.

"Lucky to be alive?"

"Ha no, but yes, that too," she said. "She told me I'm lucky to have someone like you, someone who cooks with me and spends time in nature with me. I'm just lucky to be with someone who lets me be my real self."

"That's the nicest thing you could say," I said. I handed her one of the orange flowers.

"It's true," she said.

"Yeah, I feel the same way. And it's more than all that, too," I said.

"Way more," she said.

There was flashing in the fog above treetops. Muffled bangs rang off the hills and the glass facades of the university buildings nearby.

"Shit! What was that?" I asked.

A subsequent series of light bursts were followed by another chorus of booms. Immediately, the dogs could be heard howling all around the neighborhood.

"Guess what today is?" she asked. "Babe, it's the Fourth of July!"

Stinging Nettle

(URTICA DIOICA)

Blanch before eating. Save broth for soups and teas. Wear gloves. We filled a contractor bag with nettles in Hickory Hill. We'd frozen some of the broth and I thawed it out for soup.

"Nettle broth is an anti-inflammatory," I said.

"Says who?" she asked.

"My childhood best friend, Jude. Have I told you about Jude?"

"Remind me."

"He's the one who teaches upstate, awesome wife, the cutest daughter."

"And they met at your friend's wedding?"

"Yeah, they met at the wedding and were doing the long distance thing. They didn't plan it, but she called and told him she was pregnant, so he just left work, got in his car, and drove straight to Vermont right then and said to her: okay, let's do this."

"You love that story."

"I do, Jude's the man."

Dear Catalpa,

I'm freezing. I'm wearing two pairs of SmartWools, two hats, I haven't left my bed in two days. I'm projecting a movie onto my bedroom wall, a movie I made in my mind.

It's May in my movie, she's making her onscreen debut, snapping off bites of raw asparagus for the camera. Next scene: the close-up of a bee, pollen-dusted and working over a purple coneflower with the sound of her laughter, a bibulous sea of light.

June: she's making popcorn in a cast-iron on the stove-top with her sister, who listens and laughs and jostles the oiled kernels over the flame. Her head rests in her mother's lap, on the couch in her old apartment. They share the same movements as they nod and talk with their hands.

July: we ascend a wooded path at the palisades, her first day with the sling off. We go out for a celebratory dinner. That night she's sore and we soak in the tub. In bed, I comb her scalp, sift through her wet hair in search of ticks that aren't there.

Almost August: we pass into the river of sleep. The boughs of the willows dip down to drink, and iridescent moths touch down on our bodies, hitching a ride on our foreheads and chests until the sound of the approaching falls sends them fluttering off. We float on, the birds in the trees have quieted, and the roar of the falls mounts in a towering curtain of white noise, but we still lie there. We can't hear anything over the beating of our hearts.

Purple Coneflower

(ECHINACEA PURPUREA)

"Darlin', we need to be extra safe."

"Why?"

"Because I spent all day hanging out with my coworker's baby, and I think I'm getting baby fever."

FOUR

"On prayer-meeting night, outside / the vestibule among multiple /
bell-pulls of Virginia creeper, / the terrible clepsydra of becoming /
distills its drop: a luna moth, the emblem / of the born-again, furred like an orchid /
behind the ferned antennae, a totem- / garden of lascivious pheromones, /
hangs, its glimmering streamers / pierced by the dripstone burin of the eons /
with the predatory stare out of the burrow, / those same eyeholes. Imago /
of unfathomable evolvings, living / only to copulate and drop its litter, /
does it know what it is, what it has been, / what it may or must become?"

—AMY CLAMPITT

LUNA MOTH CLUNG to the window screen, intermittently beating its chartreuse wings, and she said, "I'm late."

There was a night, the month prior, on the full moon, when we went for a walk in the cemetery, and she grabbed my crotch.

"I'm really fucking hard," I said.

"Well, I'm really fucking wet."

"What are doing here then? My place, let's run!"

We fell on my bed together, glossed with sweat and saliva and cum, talking and touching until we were ready again. She writhed prone, gripping the wood spokes of my headboard as it banged against the wall. My tits sagged, I was sweating so much, but when I was with her, I just felt less ashamed of my body. I was able to really let go. She started to come and I came.

She followed me downstairs, humming that Donnie and Joe Emerson song that Ariel Pink covered. I peed outside off the back porch and I could hear her going beyond the ajar bathroom door. We popped some LaCroixs. She burped and we laughed.

"Sorry," she said.

"You mean 'Sorry, I meant to puke,'" I said.

She laughed.

"My dad taught us to say that, our mom hated it."

"What would your parents think of me?"

"You'd dazzle them, just burp just like that."

Moonlight illuminated the kitchen. She searched the cupboard for a vase, and a crescent of her bare butt appeared from under the hem of her t-shirt. I was still hard somehow. She stuck a few boughs of white flowers into the vase, filled it with water, and arranged them on the table. As I reached for two more seltzers in the fridge, I felt her lips on the back of my skull.

Upstairs, huddled together in bed, I had a false-awakening dream. The bedroom was bathed in an indigo haze. I couldn't find my glasses, but I knew there was something in the room with us: a baby. I jumped out of bed to investigate. Sifting through the hamper of dirty clothes and ducking under the bed turned up nothing. I moved books and magazine from the floor, pulled the drafting table away from the wall, brushed aside the dust bunnies and socks and yellowed tissues, but the baby seemed to have disappeared. I was moving too slowly in this dream; I felt as if I were trudging through water. I heard the baby, though, scuttling along the baseboards, but it still managed to elude me.

Finally, exhausted, I retreated for the bed. And that's when I saw it: the baby sitting at the top of the stairs.

In the morning, she asked, "What did you dream about?"

"It's weird. I haven't been remembering my dreams lately," I said.

"Me neither," she said.

"I'm late. I'm fucking late. I'm broken and I might be pregnant," she said.

I wasn't sure what reaction she wanted from me, so I tried out acting assured. "Okay, okay. Like, how late are we talking?"

She crumpled onto the bed and rolled her face into her pillow, then turned to me. "Three days," she said, and frowned.

"Three days," I repeated. "Okay, well, do you think it could have something to do with the accident and the trauma and everything? It could be the painkillers? Hydrocodone, those super big ibuprofen they gave you — those could certainly affect these sort of things. Right? I'm just thinking out loud."

"No, I know. I don't know," she said.

I opened my laptop and Googled a list of the side effects associated with her medication. "Here, look, 'Side effects include missed, late, or irregular menstruation.'" I said.

"Yeah. Yeah, that makes sense. It's probably the meds. I don't know why I'm freaking out about this. Sometimes it's just late, it happens," she said. She wiggled under the covers and pulled the comforter up to her chin. She squeezed my hand, and kissed it. "Sweetest boyfriend," she said.

She was asleep, and I reached over her and plugged in our phones, turned off the light. In the window, the silhouette of a back-lit luna moth.

We weren't convinced. I bet she'd had a feeling for a while, before her late cycle, that *something* was happening. There'd been signs. Her breasts were sore, but I suggested it could be that her immobilizer was too tight, maybe her sling was causing the irritation. Our sex had changed, morphed from something aggressive and hot into something intimate and dreamy, a slow ritual. But I thought that, too, could be chalked up to the meds, or her fragility as a result of all the broken bones.

The one thing I couldn't explain away though, was the glow.

I always heard people say pregnant women have "a glow about them," but I never took it seriously. I wondered what this "glow" would actually entail. Beatific halos or woo-woo auras in lavender and turquoise? But I kid you not, the glow is real. Not a visible apparition, but a physical heat radiating from her body; she was hot to the touch. In her sleep she'd unconsciously seek me under the covers, pull my arm around her, and I'd feel this warm light coursing under her skin. And that's when I knew, with that subterranean instinct, that deeply animal part of us all that detects the things our rational brain works to ignore. I knew the two of us were not alone.

Scarlet Tanager

(PIRANGA OLIVACEA)

*In Spillville, Dvorak heard tanagers singing their sundown songs;
they broke his heart, inspired his "Quartet for Strings No. 12; The
American." He'd come all the way from Bohemia by way of New
York, and after only three days in Iowa, he began making music.
When I was hoping our luck would change, I listened to the second
movement, the lento, the tune borrowed from a Kickapoo funeral
song. I was eager for the third, the molto vivace to arrive, and the
exuberant finale, but whatever recording I'd downloaded ended
with the string lament.*

Dear Catalpa,

Logical explanations don't mean much to the heart. For instance, there is no way to explain why I can't bring myself to play "Turn Your Radio On" by the Blue Sky Boys for you. It's a roots country track, and when I taught fifth grade back in Brooklyn, my kids were really into this kind of music. At least, I played a lot of it, and they didn't complain much.

In my past life as a grade-school teacher, my favorite unit to teach was, without rival, paleontology. Not surprisingly, I was way into all things prehistoric when I was a kid. Your mother, too, was known to illustrate epic dinosaur dramas in marker in crayon. I bet you're a fan of the "terrible lizards." Perhaps there is, wherever you are, a mobile of soaring pterosaurs and parasaurolophuses suspended above you.

I once discovered the complete sun-bleached skeleton of a small sea turtle on an island off the Florida coast. I carried it with me on the flight back to New York, but only after I convinced the TSA agent that I was a fifth-grade science teacher, and the turtle bones were for my students. Now a sea turtle is not a dinosaur, I know, but they're descendants of prehistoric marine reptiles that were contemporaries of the dinos, so I feel that counts for something. To kick off the paleontology unit, I placed the turtle bones in a Rubbermaid tub, buried them with sand, and designated part of the classroom as a dig site that one of my students made a sign for: *DIGGING IN PROGRESS*. I illustrated handouts of saurischians and ornithischians, the geologic timescale. I found my trilobites and my black megalodon tooth in the supply closet, and displayed them prominently on my desk.

"How do they know the exact time when the meteor hit?" One of my students wanted to know.

"They can see it in the rocks," I said. "In the rocks that mark the end of the cretaceous and the beginning of the tertiary."

All that death appears on the fossil record as an ashen black scar in the layers of sediment; where the rock is exposed, it's visible to the naked eye.

Sometimes when in the blast radius of some catastrophic act, even the most quotidian things, the dumbest everyday shit will end up immortalized. Your grandparents, upon visiting Pompeii, recalled all the pigs, dogs, and toilets (never mind the human bodies and mosaics) that were preserved as a result of the eruption of Vesuvius. When I received the news that Ian died in a house fire off campus, the folding hexagonal wrench I worried in my hands is for some reason engraved into my mind, as if chipped into granite. Likewise, the old song "Turn Your Radio On," has been transfigured into one of these mummified casualties.

Could there have been a day any more humdrum? We drove my buddy Ed to the mall because he needed dress pants for a job interview. We watched him emerge from the Eddie Bauer dressing room and twist his hips to display his butt in chinos. Your mother bought a burgundy and white striped oxford from Banana Republic. I remember the purchase clearly, yet I have no memory of her ever wearing it. We dropped Ed off at his apartment, and sat in your mother's car before heading to Walgreens to buy a pregnancy test. She was five days late.

"Even the worst case scenario is not so bad," she said. "Hey."

"I'm listening," I said. I was nervous as hell, she could tell.

"If I'm pregnant, I get to go through it with you by my side. How lucky am I? Do you know how many women have to experience this alone?" She smiled at me. "Okay? No matter what, we'll get through this."

I tried to say a prayer in her kitchen. My prayer was that this day would not show up as a black mark on the timescale of our lives. It felt useless; anything I thought to say to God sounded too much like begging.

"Not looking good, babydoll," your mother called from the bathroom.

She joined me in the kitchen with the test in her hand. I asked to see it, as if I'd notice something she hadn't.

"See those two lines?" she said.

I told your mother I needed to go for a walk, and showed up on Ed's porch in a daze.

"Whoa, whoa, what the fuck happened, man?" he asked.

"I don't know," I said.

"Okay, okay. You don't have to say anything," he said.

Ed asked if your mother was okay. I nodded. He put on his sandals and we went for a walk while I told him everything.

"Maggie and I wouldn't have made it through shit like this," said Ed. "But what you two have is something different. She loves you."

When I returned, she was napping on the couch. I stretched supine on the carpet below her, she reached for my hand and pulled to her chest.

"This is my person," I said to myself. "And even if it is not what we want, some small bit of me and some small bit of her is growing inside of her, that is happening."

I took a picture of us. Yolky late afternoon light dredged through her hair, our hands locked. If I do get to take anything with me to the afterlife, if there is an afterlife, please God, let it be this photograph of the three of us. I pushed an earbud in and played a song your mother introduced me to, a song she loved, "Turn Your Radio On." I drifted off, beside her on the carpet, as The Blue Sky Boys sang, "*Some go on and we shall meet them on that hallelujah shore.*"

Well there you go; I told you I'd never play that song again, but here I am, listening to it with you now.

Megalodon

(CARCHARODON MEGALODON)

"She's pregnant."

"Oh, no. You guys aren't keeping it?"

"No, she's got an appointment at Planned Parenthood, but the soonest they can see her is August."

"Fuck, dude. Wasn't she just hit by a truck or something?"

"A van. It didn't hit her. She crashed her bike, though, real bad."

"Was she pregnant then?"

"Yeah."

"You guys are doing the right thing. I never told you this, but Julia had an abortion last winter. Let me just say, it was dark as fuck, man."

"I'll be so fucking happy when all this is behind us."

Dear Catalpa,

There's a video, a favorite, that was recorded during the Blissed Out Era, before the accident, before the pregnancy. The video was shot in Iowa on the morning I left for New York. Your mother and I walked through the mist and predawn cold of an early May Saturday. It was rare for us to be up that early; in spite of the fact that I'd become an earlyish riser in my adulthood, your mother and I would sometimes sleep in until noon. But that morning we watched the sun come up, burning hot pink like an iron through the haze. We made iced coffees and shared an empanada at the farmer's market, and then hit up Ingrid's garage sale. (I know I haven't even gotten to the video yet, and many of these details no doubt seem pedantic, but please indulge me, kid. I miss her so much tonight, and I'm feeling especially wistful.)

The video was recorded at Ingrid's. Your mother is sitting cross-legged on the floor in her living room. She's smiling at me from behind the harmonica she holds to her face. A pack of Ingrid's dogs surround her, wagging and sniffing, nudging her with their snouts. Her hair is pinned up, my orange fleece is zipped over her brown dress, and she's blowing on the harmonica with gusto, teetering from side to side as she plays. And the dogs are going nuts! I'm laughing, causing the phone to shake, and she keeps playing while the dogs whimper and yowl, their muzzles to the sky, their tails beating the floorboards, begging for mercy.

In my beat-up copy of *Cosmicomics*, there are check marks and stars in the margins of a passage that reads, "*I still look for her as soon the first silver appears in the sky, and the more it waxes, the more clearly I imagine I can see her, her or something like her, but only her, in a hundred, a thousand different vistas, she who makes the Moon the Moon and, whenever she is full, sets the dogs to howling all night long, and me with them.*"

I don't think I could have totally appreciated that when I first read it. I was eighteen when I first read Calvino, with muttonchops and Birkenstock-tanned feet. I'd never been in love or anything close to it.

While we were at our neighborhood bar over the Thanksgiving break, Zeus caught me watching the video on my phone, the one of her and the dogs.

"Buddy, come on. Why do that to yourself?" he said.

That's how most of my nights were ending up, with me drunk watching videos like that one, scrolling through our pictures, listening to our songs, listening to "Unchained Melody" on repeat. I'd become a fucking mess for sure, but that's just where I was.

I should tell you what else Rabbi Gold told me. He said part of loving you and your mother means being willing to stop carrying the two of you. And then he shared this story about a monk and his disciple that came upon a woman and her baby waiting beside a river, unable to cross. The monk lifted the woman and her kid onto his back, waded into the current, and forded them across the river. As the monk and his disciple walked on, the disciple was troubled.

The disciple said, "Teacher, how was it that you were able to pick up that woman?"

It was the law among those monks that they were never to touch or be touched by a member of the opposite sex.

The monk replied, "Student, I left that woman and her child back at the river's edge. It sounds as if you're the one who is still carrying them."

"Mourn," said Rabbi Gold. "And please understand that it's

appropriate for our people to mourn, but know too that at some point, you may have to stop carrying them."

I am sorry to disappoint the Rabbi, but right now I feel unable to leave you or her at the riverside.

St. Maggie Nelson, patron of the brokenhearted, wrote, *For to wish to forget how much you loved someone and then to actually forget, can feel at times like the slaughter of a beautiful bird who chose, by nothing short of grace, to make a habitat of your heart.* I'll keep writing to you, I'll keep drawing for you and telling you stories, I'll keep watching that video, I'll keep listening to "Unchained Melody."

After we knew for certain that she was pregnant, her morning sickness took on the characteristics of a horrible flu. We spent the weeks leading up to her appointment mostly in bed, watching Miyazaki and whatever nature documentaries were on Netflix. She seemed to be getting over the worst of it; she was keeping food down and had enough energy to do the exercises her physical therapist had recommended, so we invited her sister over. We cooked her dinner and streamed *Fifth Element* (which holds up, by the way). After her sister left, we started fooling around on the couch.

"Wait, wait," I said, and grabbed my phone.

"Don't ruin this!" she said. "I need it!"

"Mood music," I said.

"We don't need mood music, I'm already in the mood, just get over here."

"Unchained Melody" started playing from my phone.

"I've always loved this song," she said.

"Ditto."

Your aunt Ruth owned this CD called *Movie Love*. I stole it from her room and listened to it until the disc was so scratched up it quit playing altogether. We were playing badminton in our yard when I told your aunt "Take My Breath Away" by Berlin was my favorite track on that album.

"Nice try," said Ruth. "But that cannot be your favorite."

It couldn't be my favorite because it was *her* favorite. I conceded, and chose "Unchained Melody" as my favorite instead. I listened to my new favorite song that night in the backyard, sitting on a carpet of grass and dandelions with my CD walkmen in my lap. The Righteous Brothers' rendition of "Unchained Melody" revealed its worth to me even at age eight, an appreciation that has only grown with time.

I was a fellow that summer at a writing conference in Sun Valley, Idaho, and the last night I decamped early from a party thrown in the nearby town of Ketchum. The party was at the residence of one of the conference's benefactors. My reading that morning was a hit, the food at the party was killer, catered by some James Beard pop-up chef, and the people were all super kind. As socially inclined as I appear to most, I am, in fact, in my heart a more saturnine and contemplative creature, and that night I just did not have the energy for schmoozing. I had a lot on my mind, plus I was sober again. I sipped tonic and wandered through the tall rows of hollyhocks in the host's gardens, but then ghosted on the party, heading back for my hotel room along the unlit county road. More than anything though, that whole time I was in Idaho, I missed her: knocked-up, with her broken bones, alone back in Iowa.

The moon was a thin cold crescent, a waxing rind of light awash in a river of bright stars and far-off galaxies: a nocturn panorama unlike any I'd seen. She once said no one can claim to have seen the stars until they've seen them out west, and she was right. I called her and described everything I saw: Hercules, Scorpio, bright red Antares, all of it shining above the jagged silhouettes of the mountains.

"I'm seeing it all," she said. "It's cloudy here. What can I trade you?"

"You could sing me a song?" I suggested. "Any song, the birthday song, it doesn't matter."

"Deal," she said.

She sang me "Unchained Melody" and I sat down in the middle of the road, feeling especially small under a canopy of shining heaven. "I'll be coming home, wait for me, wait for me," she sang in a falsetto, soft and gossamer-like. She sang it all the way through, really went for it at the ending, and I would take her version over any other.

But why tire myself attempting to recreate this scene, when you know perfectly well how it was that night. From the Iowa prairie to where I stood high up in those Idaho mountains, on that night, she sang to us both.

Osprey

(PANDION HALIAETUS)

Osprey pairs collaborate on the structure of their nests and the materials used to build them. In Connecticut, I saw an osprey nest built with hula hoops; another, on Shelter Island, crafted entirely from blue rope. In addition to salvaging the materials, the male does the hunting. He dives into the water to lock his talons into a fish. A biologist buddy told me — and maybe he's full of shit — that sometimes, a big enough blue or a striper will plunge to the bottom with an osprey along for the ride. And sometimes they're found like that: the drowned bird and the dead fish, locked together in the fatal act.

.

FIVE

"Still, I'd like to see the river of stars / fall noiselessly
through the nine heavens for once, / But the world's weight, and
the world's welter speak big talk / and big confusion."
—CHARLES WRIGHT

I WAS SUPPOSED TO GO to Idaho for a fellowship in July, but during the Blissed Out Era, I wasn't thinking too much about the future. With everything else that was going on, I'd nearly forgotten about the fellowship altogether. I'd received and spent the honorarium check, but when the time came to consider my plans for the trip, I just didn't feel up for it. Truth being, I wasn't up for much of anything then; things were heavy leading up to the abortion.

We were at the Goodwill. I was losing weight rapidly and needed a pair of swim trunks that would fit.

"On my bike tour, Idaho was by far the most beautiful of all the landscapes," she said as we browsed the racks. "The mountains look like sleeping lions. You'll see. You're going to love Idaho."

"I wish you could come, too."

"I'll be okay, my mom is coming down, and Ingrid's here."

The morning of my flight, she toasted me some sourdough and reviewed my packing list again. Ingrid arrived and I demonstrated how to fasten her into her immobilizer.

When Ingrid stepped outside to make a phone call, she turned to me. "You need to be a father."

"Grazie mille."

"I meant it."

I watched Ingrid tug absent mindedly at the tendrils of one of our cucumbers on the veranda.

"If this had happened a year into our relationship," she said, "if this had happened at any other time, I want you to know that I would have kept it."

"Me too," I said.

"It would be crazy for us to keep it though, right?"

"You just started this new job. And the opiates."

"I know, I know," she said. She chewed her fingernails. "I mean, if we had a blind kid, I just, I don't know, I would never forgive myself."

The drive from Boise to Sun Valley looked like the landscape of another planet. Vast fields of igneous rubble gave way to jagged mountain ranges. Before this, the only view of the Rockies I'd seen was through the frost-covered porthole of an airplane window.

I checked in at the chalet-style lodge of the resort, registered for a hike and a fly fishing tour, and took note of all of the photos of former guests hanging in the grand hall: Katherine Hepburn and the Kennedys, Hemingway in snowshoes, Hemingway with a stringer full of steelhead, Hemingway kneeling with a slain bull elk.

Among the Pulitzer Prize and National Book Award winners, Poet Laureates and recipients of just about any other literary prize one could imagine at the welcome party, I felt understandably invisible, but to tell you the truth, that shit doesn't really get to me. Many of the other writers though, had brought along their spouses and partners, their kids, and for that I envied them. I wished, so badly, that she could have been there with me, too.

At dinner the first night, beneath the glowing tents on the grounds of one of the benefactor's summer homes, the creator of a popular crime podcast told me I couldn't sit with her, that there was no room for me at her table. I took my dinner alone on the lawn and then wandered to the banks of a creek shaded in aspens at the edge of the property. The creek bed was carpeted in smooth black stones. I scooped up two, nearly perfectly round ones, and put them in my bag to bring back for her.

After dinner, with the reception in full swing, I snooped around the house. There was a corky Milton Avery still life of citruses in the formal dining room, and a stunner of a Fairfield Porter, a farm landscape, hung above the mantle in the den. Someone said there was a Hopper upstairs in one of the bedrooms, one of his Long Island gas stations, but I didn't make it up to see. I snapped a photo of a photo of the host in Kente cloth posing alongside Nelson Mandela, and one of a Christmas card from Governor Schwarzenegger and his family that was stuck to the fridge. I was texting them to her when I was interrupted by a woman grabbing me by the bicep. Her fingers felt cold on my arm; I looked down and noted her turquoise painted nails and silver rings. She recognized me as "the bird guy" from earlier. That morning I'd helped her identify a meadowlark on the resort grounds. She was the wife of a former secretary of the treasury. She said I just had to meet her friend, who was also a birder and also the wife of another former secretary of the treasury. "Stay right here," she said, and went to fetch her friend. As soon as she was swallowed by the party, I split.

I hid out in the bathroom and Facetimed her back in Iowa.

"This place sounds weird," she said.

"It's weird," I agreed. "It's fancy as hell. I think I'm making friends, though."

"Don't make too many friends," she said. "You'll never come back to Iowa! I love that pic you sent, by the way."

"The Governator or the sego lily?" I asked.

"The one of you holding the sego lily," she said. "Have you always been the sweetest thing?"

One of the new friends I'd made, a Texan writer, coerced the event staff into granting us a tour of the hunting lodge where Hemingway died. On the drive up, I mentioned that that day also happened to be Hemingway's birthday.

"Spooky," my Texan friend replied.

The lodge was on a dirt road high over Ketchum. It was left to the Nature Conservancy fifty years ago, and they still hadn't figured out what to do with the property, the home, or any of the junk in it.

"We were thinking this lodge could serve as a residency for emerging writers," the archivist said.

A macabre suggestion.

"Yeah, I don't see why not," I replied.

On the wall, there was a Polaroid of the dead author, bare-assed on the deck of his boat somewhere off Cuban waters, and other photographs of his different wives and lovers. An antelope head was mounted on the fieldstone hearth; Hem shot it, as well as another smaller mount that Mary, his fourth wife, took. Handpainted Majorcan tiles lined the wainscoting. The floors were flocked with wall-to-wall carpeting woven with colors of blood and gold. Over the stairs hung an oil painting of a bull being skinned following a bullfight — a birthday present, we were told. Sport coats and trousers hung in the cedar closet. Atop the black steamer trunk was a dusty pair of his boots along with his tennis racket. A ribbon was in the typewriter, a razor and a shaving brush were in the medicine cabinet. Each window sill was ornamented with crystals and mammal skulls, songbird eggs, feathers and fossils from his hikes through the Sawtooths. It didn't feel like a museum; if anything, it was a tomb. She'd love this place.

My phone began to ring; it was her. I slipped through the same entryway where Hemingway finally propped his rifle, took aim, and brought down his charging mind. From the veranda, three separate mountain ranges converged within view.

"Guess who else is pregnant?" she asked. Her voice was fractured.

Ingrid, her best friend, was as far along as she was.

"She's going to keep it," she said. A fissure of tears trembled in her voice. "I don't know how they're going manage."

"I'll be home in the morning," I said. "Stay at my house tonight, you know where the key is."

"Okay, I know. I'm sorry for ruining whatever it is you're doing now."

"No, don't apologize, please. You didn't ruin anything. I'm coming home."

Zeus was waiting for me at O'Hare. He noticed that I was scribbling compulsively on the notebook in my lap.

"Novel or short story?" he asked.

"Neither, it's trash," I said.

What I was writing was a sad and dorky Tanka. I was too embarrassed to share it with Zeus or anyone. Here it is anyway:

> *An osprey, broken*
> *winged, remains on an egg*
> *she can't bear to hatch.*
> *Her mate does circles above*
> *mountains. Oh, his poor bird heart.*

Sego Lily

(CALOCHORTUS NUTTALLII)

Hopis picked these mountain flowers for new mothers. Utes ground the bulbs for porridge. He prayed this prayer to himself as the plane took flight from Boise: if I'm the reason she doesn't want to keep this baby, please let this plane crash in some ranch in Wyoming. Let me be the only casualty. Let me be a father only in memory, so she can be a mother in this life. Amen.

Dear Catalpa,

*What do you get when you cross twelve sticks of dynamite with a little
French emperor?*

    Napoleon Blownaparte.

    That joke and the drawings it inspired were favorites from my
childhood. Your uncle and I would illustrate issues of our comic,
The Untold Stories of Napoleon Blownaparte. The series enjoyed
a lengthy run. We even shot silkscreens of our favorite panels, pin-
holing the negative image of an exploding Napoleon: his intestines
strung through the air like streamers, his bones, tiny hands, boots,
and bicorne hat all incinerated in the blast along with his enemies.
But following each explosion, in the next frame, the little general
would be reassembled, mounted on his steed and charging toward
his next battle.

    Today I feel wedged — crushed, really — somewhere between
those two frames. Maybe it's because I swear I saw you today, or

at least a child like the one you could've been. Her parents walked on ahead, as she talked to her shadow and brushed a stick over the snow. She looked up at me, and I swear she shared my complexion, my lips, your mother's eyes, chin, her thick dark hair. This exploding chest exploded again.

Indian Blanket

(SUN VALLEY, IDAHO)

Ruby sunflower petals chrome yellow tipped. Pass through the desert at dusk; a garnet sun flowers, hammers arroyos in goldleaf. Cottonwoods snow cotton dander in bolts. I'm lifting your body over the dust of a dry river.

SIX

 HE LEFT FOR THE APPOINTMENT at Planned
Parenthood by herself. I offered to go with, but she
said I didn't need to.

"Do you know what would be a big help, though?"

"Anything," I said.

"Just spend these next few days with me, just the two of us, no
matter how shitty I am," she said. "Can you do that?"

"I already got off from work," I said. "We'll screen a *Lord of the
Rings* marathon, extended versions. I've already downloaded them."

"Yes!" she said.

"I'll get all the snacks from the co-op. If you can dream it, we'll
eat it," I said. "Bumble Bars, Annie's pizzas, jalapeño cashew spread
by the gallon, pimento cheese, all the LaCroixs."

"Yes," she said. "My hero!"

RU-486, the abortion pill, is expensive. Almost $500, which isn't the most money, but $500 might as well be $5,000 for most of the people who need it. We needed it, and it was more money than we had. I was broke and we really couldn't ask our parents for help. Nearly nobody knew she was pregnant anyhow; we were going through it mostly alone, mostly unspoken, even between ourselves, mostly in the dark.

I had a year contract as an adjunct professor, and the job only paid during the academic year. Each summer I had to get creative, taking on all kinds of work to scrape together something that resembled an income. I worked at the museum store, selling Herman Miller office chairs and Saarinen tables, Danish mobiles and cheese graters of Italian design, but they stopped giving me shifts after I left for Idaho. I worked construction for a friend of a friend, taking a rental property down to the studs, but I quit after they expected me to pry up asbestos tiles. So I took on more freelance assignments at the Cedar Rapids newspaper and on weekends I had a gig helping to paint a mural outside the co-op. I served as an airport greeter for a summer writing program, worked front-of-house at my buddy's food truck, and helped him with catering gigs, too. But during the week I dug potatoes and pulled garlic at an organic farm. The farm work wasn't easy, but it was consistent, and it paid cash. At the end of each day, the farm manager gave me a wad of money, which I in turn unfolded, bill by bill, and handed over to her when I got home.

"I feel like I'm in a Steinbeck novel," I said, the night before the abortion.

She laughed.

"I'm seeing garlic stalks," I said. "When I close my eyes, I see the film negatives of garlic stalks sliding by. I see my gloved hands pulling them. It's all projected on the undersides of my eyelids, like those floating dust motes you get on your eyes, you know? Or I guess like the visuals you get when you're on mushrooms."

"Totally," she said. "That used to happen to me all the time when I was a kid, in the summers when I was detasseling corn. I'd be in bed, so exhausted and just as I was falling asleep these visions of corn stalks would appear, I'd see my hands reaching out for them."

"When we do have a kid, it'd be nice to raise them in the Pacific Northwest or something. Maybe the Hudson Valley, or Vermont," I said. "New Mexico."

"Or Iowa," she said. "Iowa is perfect."

It was 4:00 p.m. when she got home from her appointment, and I noticed a change right away. I watched as she dumped her bag on the kitchen chair, slid her shoes off one at a time. She acted like she was performing some dance in a daze, her whole body seemed to be cast in shadow. She mechanically fished a bobby pin from her pocket, filled a glass with water. I stood in the doorway. I wasn't even sure she noticed me until she walked up, slumped her head on my shoulder, and took me by the hand and led me to her bed.

"I have to take the second pill tomorrow," she said.

"Okay," I said.

"The ultrasound technician asked me if I wanted to know if it was twins," she said, and pulled the covers over her head.

"Was it?" I asked.

"No," she said, her voice muffled. "There was this crazy old man, though," she continued, lifting the blanket from her head. "He tried to block me from entering the parking lot. He stood in front of my car, but then finally moved. As soon as I got out, he shoved this Xeroxed picture of an aborted fetus in my face. He kept saying, 'Do you see this? Isn't she beautiful?'"

"I'm going to find him, and I'm going to fucking kill him," I said. "I'm going to find him and beat the fucking life out of him."

"Stop," she said, gently. "You know he wouldn't be there doing what he's doing if he didn't believe in it."

"That's fine. I'm still going to break his fucking neck."

"Yes, you're very strong," she said. "But please, please, just stop talking like that."

Neither of us said anything for several minutes. I got up and found some drawing paper and good pens. I started drawing and then she did, too. I drew these cartoony phantoms and pterodactyls and she began drawing tiny cell-like circles.

"You want Indian, don't you?" I asked.

She nodded.

I phoned in an order for chana saag and bharta and garlic naan and biked out to pick it up. When I left she was making these tiny crenellations like teeth on the edge of her paper, rows and rows, filling the page. I was biking back, with our dinner swinging from our handlebars, when someone shouted hello to me. It was the couple that lived on our street; we'd become friendly with them and even expressed abstract plans about meeting up for dinner sometime. They were our age, and they had an infant son with Down syndrome. The last time we spotted them pushing their stroller down the next block, she suggested we turn at the corner. "I just don't want to talk to them right now," she said. I pretended not to hear them, and I biked fast past them on my way back home.

When I returned with our food, she was still drawing teeth. Without looking up, she said, "What am I supposed to learn from this?"

Halfway through *The Fellowship of the Ring*, her phone chimed. She checked it and stared at the screen blankly.

"What is it?" I asked.

She held the phone so we both could see. It was a video of Ingrid and her man, the baby daddy, at the doctor's office for the ultrasound. A gray blob pulsed on the monitor. The doctor was talking. Ingrid laughed. The gray blob wiggled, and the video ended on a selfie, a shot of the mother and father. When it was over, she placed her phone on the nightstand.

"We'd be such better parents," she said. "They fight constantly."

"Wow," I said, involuntarily. "They looked so happy."

"Well, of course they do," she said, and started to cry. "It's a fucking miracle."

Garlic

(ALLIUM SATIVUM)

Music, Russian Red, Ukrainian, and one unwelcome variety.
Bulbs, already clipped, regrow stalks in crates in the hoop house.
Laughter was a song that stopped being played on this farm after
the hand burned the silo down. Swallowing raw cloves is said to
prevent ghosts from inhabiting the hollow parts growing inside you.

Dear Catalpa,

I just got back to New York, and I had a panic attack on the D train today. I was leaving Ruth's on my way to the Brooklyn Museum; I had a dream about Jusepe de Ribera's painting, "Saint Joseph with the Flowering Rod," and needed to go see it. While rattling along the elevated portion of the line near the Green-Wood Cemetery, watching a brown liquid roll and retreat in a tide across the train car floor, I began to feel strangely lightheaded and hot in the face. It felt like an electric current coursing under my skin. This sensation, which began in my ears and jaw, grew until my whole body felt tingly and bloodless. I snapped my eyelids shut and clenched my fists as if it might help. "I have to get off this train," I thought.

A man in puffy coat and a Giants cap leaned over me. "Sir, you need to get off? Want me to get the conductor?"

"No, it's okay," I said. I must've been thinking out loud. "Thank

you, no I'm fine. I have low blood sugar is what it is, but I'll be fine."
I sifted through my bag and produced a Clif Bar. "See?"

"All right, but if you need something," he said, and sat back
down.

A woman and her two daughters who were seated next to me got
up and moved to the far end of the car. The train went underground
and the feeling subsided.

In August, I took a shortcut home through the woods behind the art
library, and bursting forth ecstatically from the base of a shagbark
hickory was a stand of tall pink flowers. The stems were limber green
wands, each one erupting in six, ten, a dozen trumpeting blossoms:
the manifold heads of a floral hydra. I had stumbled upon a patch
of the summer's first nerines.

I'll draw you a nerine, but if I were to paint you one instead,
I'd start with a pat of titanium white and cut in a dab of alizarin
crimson. I'd fold in a pallet knife's edge of ultramarine blue for the
pale magenta petals, a brush tip of chrome yellow. More white, cad
yellow, venetian red, and burnt umber to grant form to the flamboy-
ant stamens. I'll paint you nerines next summer, I promise, when
they're in bloom.

I asked the nerines I found that day for pardon, and severed several stalks from the stand.

"You're for my sweetheart," I said. "She needs you. I hope you understand."

I filled a vase, arranged the blooms, and left them on the island in the kitchen. I filled a juice glass with water, so she, upstairs in bed, could take the second pill. I paused, filled another glass, slipped one of the nerines in it, and carried that up as well.

When I finally made it to the Brooklyn Museum, I bolted straight up to the European wing to see the de Ribera. Standing before the dark oil portrait of the father of Christ, one could trace de Ribera's hand down through Velasquez, Goya. Joseph's shoulders are square with the gilded frame while his head is turned in profile, his chin angled up as if raised by the finger of an invisible hand. He's garbed in black, and wrapped in goldenrod-colored cloak. One gaunt hand hovers over his breast, the other clutches a wooden staff from which bloom daffodils, lilies, and roses.

In my notebook, I began sketching the composition in graphite. An Eastern European woman, about seventy, with dyed black hair and denim overalls, peeked over my shoulder. I took a half step away from her, pushed my glasses onto the top of my head, squinted at the canvas. I held my pencil up, taking measurements, scanning back and forth between the painting and my drawing.

"Yours looks different," she said.

"Uh huh," I said, and kept sketching.

"What kind of flowers are those in your drawing?"

"Nerines," I said. "Every last one of them is a nerine."

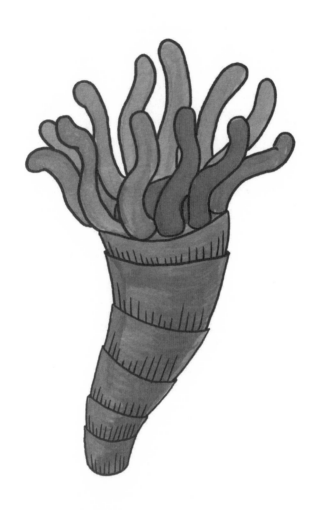

Horned Coral

(CORALVILLE, IOWA)

Iowa is fossil country; take Coralville, named for the horned corals
the earth spits up like arrowheads from the soil. The horn is a calyx,
is a calcium carbonate shell of extinct cnidaria, though nothing
remains of the invertebrate bodies. Nimble tentacles quivered in
Silurian seas, today soil's rolled in asphalt, malls outshine fireflies
flashing their bodies in the tall grass teeming in an off-ramp ditch.

SEVEN

I'M NOT THE KIND OF GIRL who makes out in Clark's," she said.

But that was where we first kissed, in the ruby glow of a neon Pabst sign at Clark's. We'd spent hours sitting on the same side of the booth. I listened, rapt as she talked. I'm not sure I was able to conceal how blown away I was by her that night, how fascinated I was by her stories of bike tours and dinners she'd catered. I loved the way she spoke affectionately of her friends, her family. We passed napkins back and forth, playing exquisite corpse as the space between us shrank — knee touching knee, hand grazing hand, hands held, mouths locked.

I spent a long time lost in this memory of our first date while I sat with Doc on the bench outside of St. Mary's. I'd hardly been listening to anything he was saying.

"So I'm banned for life!" he said. "From Clark's Buffet, if you can believe that shit!"

"Say, Doc," I said. "What do you know about RU-486?"

"You mean the abortion pill? I know quite a bit," said Doc. "Actually, I could tell you just about anything you want to know about it."

A retired Army doctor, Doc was for decades the lone physician performing abortions at the Iowa City Women's Clinic, the second of its kind in the country. He's told me stories about attempts on his life, shots fired at him by the Catholics. They missed, twice. He also claimed to have performed an abortion for Patty Hearst while she was on the lam. Much to his pleasure, and largely due to his own efforts, he's something of a local legend. He's also a legendary drunk. Most days, he holds court on the benches outside St. Mary's Roman Catholic Church, sipping beer from a Hawkeyes coffee mug.

"It was developed by the French," he said. "It's given in the form of two separate pills. The first pill, the progesterone inhibitor, they have you take right there at the clinic. The second, the one that induces the soft muscle contractions, causing the actual miscarriage, that one is usually taken at home."

My friend Lily confided in me about her abortion. She had undergone a surgical procedure, not the pill; she had just wanted it to be over. The father was in Barcelona, and she had no intention of being a single mother at twenty-five.

"Why would any woman choose to take the second pill at home? Why drag it out?" she asked the doctor.

"There are a few good reasons," the doctor replied. "But generally, it's because they'd prefer to be at home, with their loved ones, during what can be a difficult process."

"Oh, God," said Lily. "It didn't even occur to me that some women don't have to go through this all completely alone, like I had to."

I was there when my loved one took her second pill. I watched her swallow it. I saw her check her phone to mark the time; in an hour, it would begin. I read her the Planned Parenthood pamphlet and then read her some Dune. She gripped my hand as desperately as though she were dangling from the rim of canyon. I have witnessed in my life few things so awful as the fear and sorrow I saw frozen in her eyes, as she trembled in bed, waiting for the end to begin.

Doc smeared the sweat from his brow with the back of his liver-spotted hand.

"What's eating you, buddy? Something is, I can tell," he said.

"My girlfriend took the pill, Doc. She took RU-486, a few weeks ago," I said.

"Was it yours?" asked Doc.

I nodded.

"I'm sorry," he said. "Oh, wow. I'm very sorry, buddy. How old is she?"

"Twenty-six," I said. "She'll be twenty-seven next week."

"When you're a kid in high school in this situation, it's a no-brainer. But the older you get, it's a tougher call to make. How's she holding up?" he asked.

"Okay, I think. She seems kind of down and kind of out of it, but also kind of relieved, too. She was in a really horrible bike accident when she was first pregnant."

"Oh fuck, I'm sorry," he said. He touched my shoulder.

"She hasn't kissed me since the abortion," I said. I started to cry.

"Believe it or not, that sounds about right. It's a nasty little pill, screws with their pituitary gland. She'll come back though. You love her?" asked Doc.

"More than anything," I said.

"I was going to say, because this could be a good time for you to duck out, if you know, if you've got leaving on your mind," said Doc.

"No. Things like this bring people closer, it doesn't tear them apart," I said.

"Well, then hang in there, for her. It won't be easy, but just be there. Treat her like your sister. When she does come around, and she will, she'll be glad that you stood by her through it all."

"Thank you."

I got up. Doc hauled himself up from the bench, too, and drained the contents of his mug.

I left feeling emboldened and lighter, but as I biked away the heaviness and worry became to settle over me again like the settling of spores. Doc could have performed a million abortions, but he'd never had one himself. What then did he actually know about what she was going through? And what did I really know either?

Hen of the Woods

(GRIFOLA FRONDOSA)

I was seized by the stupid superstition that if I somehow found her a hen of the woods mushroom she'd start loving me again.

Dear Catalpa,

In the hit single from their legendary sophomore album *The Score*, the Fugees' Lauren Hill describes a woman at a concert watching a musician render, with uncanny accuracy, the portrait of her own heartbreak. She's aghast as the crowd listens to his song. *Strumming my pain with his fingers, singing my life with his words. Killing me softly with his song . . . I felt he found my letters, and read each one out loud. I prayed that he would finish, but he just kept right on,* Hill moans, and oh God, do I know how she feels.

I came of age listening to the Fugees' version of "Killing Me Softly." Later, I discovered that it was a cover of a Roberta Flack single recorded back in 1971. It can be revelatory when a song, or any other piece of art, reads like a relief map of the contours of your heart. But it's not always a pleasurable experience, since most often these songs feel more like a condemnation than what we'd actually desire: a sympathetic touch, the knowing companionship of a friend. After you departed, and I felt the love steadily dripping out of her, I'd agonize if Conway Twitty and Loretta Lynn came on the radio to tell me there *was nothing cold as ashes after the fire went out.* While she was performing her involuntary vanishing act, any country or motown song for that matter could quite literally drive me to my knees. Why is it all the good songs happen to be about heartbreak, lovesickness?

She had two birthday parties: one at her restaurant thrown by her co-workers, and a surprise party that I had planned. Our friends helped plan the surprise, and we staked out a pavilion at the park on the palisades of the Cedar River: a place she loved. Her friends, most of them farmers and bartenders and workers in the food service industry, laid out a bounty of food. On each table I set out wildflowers: echinacea, sunflowers, bee balm, and chrysanthemums of various hues. Ed found some geodes and fossils in the riverbed and arranged them with the flowers to make centerpieces that looked like the sort of naturabilia she adored.

"Prepare to get laid tonight," said Ed.

"Shut up, dude," I said. We crept around the tables, lighting candles. "I'm not worried about that. She's had the worst fucking summer of her life. She deserves a celebration."

"You've had a shitty fucking summer yourself, hombre. Don't you forget it," said Ed. "You two deserve to get each other off."

"You're right, it would be nice," I said.

Immediately after the abortion, your mother lost her libido. Physical contact seemed to make her nervous. Several nights she thanked me for not pressuring her, for understanding, for being patient, but the waiting was making me feel anxious, insecure, and undesirable. "It'll come back," she said.

"I know," I said.

She blew out the candles on her carrot cake, we lit the fireworks. Ingrid invited the guests to burn worry sticks in the bonfire. It was a beautiful night. We didn't have sex. I won't say I wasn't disappointed.

Ingrid organized party number two, a karaoke party at the restaurant. For each one of our friends, Ingrid Photoshopped psychedelic portraits she projected onto a sheet on the stage. The one for me was a photo of me in my orange beanie, with mushrooms and ferns and birds circling my head, and a baseball bat-sized spliff dangling from my lip (at that point, I hadn't smoked weed in months for fear that if I did, it would trigger a nervous breakdown). I sang Hank Williams and The Everly Brothers.

When your mother took the stage, everyone cheered. By virtue of some cruel chance, Ingrid had created an image of your mother holding our friend's baby, her body outlined in animated confetti, with cartoon babies crawling around her. She didn't seem fazed by it, so I tried to ignore it, too. She took a seat on the edge of the stage, held the mic in both hands, and gestured for everyone else to be seated. The song she chose was Dolly Parton's "I Will Always Love You," the one made famous by Whitney Houston on *The Bodyguard* soundtrack, and she fucking nailed it. Everyone went wild, clapped and whistled, while I just sat there, softly being killed. I could only interpret every lyric as her way of saying goodbye. "*We both know, I'm not what you need.*"

We were the last two left. Your mother, being the manager, was left to close even though it was her own birthday party. There she was, scrubbing glasses and settling the batch at 2:00 a.m. as I took out the garbage and recycling, unplugged the lights on the patio and swept the floors, watered the plants, flipped the signs, rinsed the taps. And then, with just the two of us alone behind the bar, she kissed me, passionately and with her whole body; it was the first time she'd come to me as a lover in nearly a month. There is no way to communicate the repose I felt in the wake of that kiss. But on the walk home, she sobbed.

"You're the best boyfriend anyone could ask for, and somehow you're mine," she said. "And here I am, the absolute worst."

"No. Things have been shitty, but you've been good to me. You haven't taken anything out on me."

"It's not like we're breaking up," she said.

"Who said that?"

"Do you love me?" she said.

"I do."

"Do you want to marry me?"

"I would."

"And you understand I live with depression?"

"Yes."

"And you still love me?"

"Yes."

"But how do you know, like really know? What if you just think you love me, because you've had to take care of me?" she asked.

I told her I trusted how I felt, and what could be truer than the truth of a feeling? It wasn't so much that we both enjoyed curing salmon and digging burdock root, listening to *Sweetheart of the Rodeo* and laughing through Lynch's disasterpiece *Dune*, but that whatever force drew us to these things was flowing from a common source. The experience of having someone understand you, to see the reflection of your hopes in another, to bear witness to the bright pith of another's being, those are the events in nature that can neither be heightened or diminished through words. All that we'd undergone seemed to reveal the unconcealed nature of her heart to me, and in that space I felt a home. So maybe I do love her, in part, because of all of the shit the two of us went through, but what is love if not the refuge we find in someone else when confronted with life's suffering?

"I don't think I love you, I feel I love you," I said. "Which is more real."

"I'm just being crazy," she said.

"You're not crazy at all. You're like the one non-crazy person in my life."

"Can you pick me up?" she asked.

"Like how?"

"Like pick me up and hold me?"

I can't be sure that I am not, at this moment, still holding her.

Chanterelle

(CANTHARELLUS CIBARIUS)

[Evening, a kitchen in a Midwestern ranch-style home. A "Savage Love" podcast can be heard on the speakers of a laptop. A woman in a brown dress is seasoning a cast-iron pan, while stopping periodically to check her phone. A man enters the kitchen by way of the back door that leads out to the yard.]

MAN: *Guess what I found growing everywhere along the trails in Hickory Hill?* [He holds a paper sack out to the woman. She doesn't move.]

MAN: *Chanterelles.*

WOMAN: *What if we're ruined? What if we're wasting each other's time?*

MAN: *What do you mean.* [He sets paper sack on table, takes seat.] *With us, nothing's wasted. We use every part of the buffalo.*

WOMAN: [She doesn't laugh, her expression is severe.] *I'm sorry you're in love with me.*

MAN: *Well, I'm not sorry at all.*

EIGHT

HE ASKED ME TO PICK UP prosciutto, cherry tomatoes, a bottle of rosé, and a brick of seltzer, preferably lime. She was hosting a scary movie night at her house, and I was happy to pick up anything; I was just glad to know this movie thing was really happening. She was riding her bike again, cooking again, and now hosting her friends. More and more, she seemed to resemble the woman I knew before the accident, before the abortion, before our days got so dark.

In the beginning, scary movies were something that really freaked her out. I coerced her into watching *Scream* one night, which I felt had enough of a camp factor to mitigate the gore and jumpy slasher parts, but she was so freaked out we turned it off. Instead, she showed me some of her favorite horror movie trailers on YouTube.

"These have just enough scary, you know?" she said.

"Most of these trailers are better than the actual movies, I'm sure," I said.

She pulled off my Giants cap and put it on her own head, clicked on another trailer.

But that late summer, she wanted to watch every scary movie we could stream or rent from the library, blockbusters and foreign, all the classics. We went to a midnight showing of some schlocky Hollywood horror film, and not ten minutes after the opening credits, she hooked her arm under my bicep; I could feel her body shaking. A knife scraped down the bedroom door, and she buried her face in my fleece, she locked her arms around me and did not let go until the credits rolled. But outside the dark mall theater, she'd hardly touch me.

There was a time when, upon seeing the two of us sleeping, it would've been difficult discerning where one of us ended and the other began in the nest of sheets. But she'd taken to curling up to her own side, and the inches between our bodies felt like an insurmountable expanse.

For scary movie night, she was showing a film she was always too frightened to watch: *The Shining*. I was at the co-op getting the snacks when Ed texted, "Please don't hate me I'm an asshole I fucked up but it's cool." I called him.

"What happened?" I asked.

"I saw her at work, I got a beer, and we were talking about scary movie night, and then for some reason I made a dead baby joke, and then I made another one."

"Jesus, Ed." I sat down on the floor in the soda aisle.

"I know, I know. But she didn't seem offended."

"It's just the littlest thing sends her down a such a dark spiral, and this isn't a little thing."

"She's a tough broad, dude. I just wanted to 'fess up in case you hear it from her. I'm still coming over for *The Shining*."

When I got home with the groceries, she was straightening up and listening to Fleetwood Mac. She actually seemed pretty upbeat. Ed was the first to arrive, followed by Ingrid and her man, also some of the ladies from her work. I balanced the wine and the glasses and a tray of roasted chanterelles as I tiptoed down the stairs.

"No wine for me, just seltzer," said Ingrid. "Pregnant lady over here!"

Her man laughed. "I'll be drinking for both of us," he said.

I looked at her, but she was busy pouring wine for our friends; their faces lit by the television set. She had saved me a seat beside her on the couch, and she wiggled her feet under my thigh, laid her head on my shoulder. Even as the Torrance's red Volkswagen Bug crawled through the mountain roads in the sweeping aerials of the opening credits, I could tell that she was seriously afraid. Danny talked to Tony, she grabbed me tighter. Danny encountered the twins in the hall, she pushed my hand between her thighs. Jack was mesmerized by the nude woman rising from the tub in the eerie green bathroom of Room 237, her hands were wet with sweat and she dug her nails deeply into my wrists. The elevator doors open, releasing a torrent of blood into the hall.

American Goldfinch

(SPINUS TRISTIS)

"Ingrid said she didn't have sex for two months after hers, and one website said it takes three months."

"Six months, ten months, ten years, it doesn't matter, I can wait."

"It's not fair to you."

"It has nothing to do with fairness."

"You're taking care of me, but who's taking care of you?"

"You are."

"Barely."

Dear Catalpa,

This past September, while we were still hanging on, I started teaching again at the Montessori school in town. It was a month-long gig, filling in for Ms. Vanessa, who was on vacation. I picked the chicken nugget debris from the carpet and got sneezed on by nine-year-olds, while she was reading a novel and sipping Caipirinhas on a beach somewhere in Brazil.

From her apartment, the bike commute to Montessori was just over five miles. The bike trail crossed the river, with the University crew boats cutting the early morning mists, then entered a segment of restored prairie adjacent to the dog park. That fall I was into this eighteenth-century commentary on the Heart Sutra, and the half mile of trails between the river and the prairie were teaming with massive, khaki grasshoppers. I shimmied and juked on my bike while the bugs vaulted directly into my path, their bodies clipped in my spokes, crunched under my tires. At least the caterpillars were easier to avoid. On my way home from school, I broke for the first wooly bear caterpillar of the season. With my bike in the grass, I inched along on my belly with my phone tilted up at a dramatic angle framing the caterpillar. The insects hissing in the weeds and the goldfinches crying in the willows provided the soundtrack for the fuzzed larva's intrepid crossing. I didn't post it to Instagram or share it with my friends, this video was for her alone.

It was October then, and she was falling out of love with me. Our cups of Iron Goddess of Mercy tea cooled on the sidewalk. I reclined in the grass, she sat checking her phone on the stoop. I asked if she'd ever watched that video I'd sent her, the one of the wooly bear.

"I did," she said. "I loved it."

"You didn't say so," I said.

"I know."

I recently told this whole anecdote to Ed and all he had to say was, "What was the ratio of brown to black on the caterpillar?"

"Who cares," I said. "She's gone, and it'll be winter forever."

"You won't always feel this way, it won't always hurt this bad," he said.

"Being away from the person I love, this hurts worse than any-thing I've felt. I wish I didn't feel this way, man, but that's just where I'm at."

"I feel that."

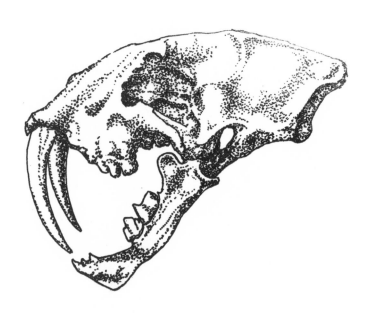

Smilodon

(WALRUS CAT)

When my student Khalil knew he'd fucked up, or pissed me off, he'd illustrate me cards to make up for it.

"I'm still mad at him," I told my co-teacher, and threw his drawing in the recycling bin.

"But he drew you his best sabertooth!" she replied.

In the end, I was pulling moves straight out of Khalil's playbook: with nothing else to lose, I stayed late at Montessori, listening to The Disintegration Loops, *and drawing her my best sabertooth.*

Dear Catalpa,

It's 3:00 in the morning. I should be asleep, I have to catch the train into DC with your grandfather in an hour, yet here I am writing you. I'm home for the holidays, though DC isn't a place I call home. My parents moved from the Catskills down to this row house in Alexandria a decade ago, and even though it's filled with all the rugs, clocks, paintings, and photographs that once decorated the old house, it's never quite felt right.

Outside my family, I don't know many people in this city anymore, but last night Lily and her husband took the train down from New York. It was a spur of the moment thing, I saw the pictures from city hall; they were leaving in a few days for a honeymoon in Vietnam. She chose the kind of place for dinner that I figured she would, a restaurant in the basement of a colonial home turned boutique hotel. I looked it up and found they offered several dozen varieties of local oysters, a fact of which they seemed quite proud, and had published a book featuring their cocktail recipes. It was the kind of place I'd lost all taste for. I buttoned up the shirt that looked the most unwrinkled and ink stain-free in my closet, and arrived early, waiting for them at the bar. When Lily arrived, she introduced me to her husband as "her dear artist friend," which made me laugh.

A dozen oysters and several drinks into the meal, Lily mentioned how she was astonished that an old friend of hers — they'd attended Brearley together — had gone to Iowa while I was there, too.

"I'm finding out that this sort of shit is more common than you'd think," I said.

"But what do you think of her art?" she asked, sawing a scallop with the side of her fork, and feeding it to her man.

"Well, she recites her work from memory, she doesn't read from her phone or anything like that, which I appreciate. And she's a really performative reader. She's got that witchy thing going on."

"Yes, but what do you think of the work?" she asked, pointing her fork at me.

Her husband grinned and excused himself to the bathroom.

"To be totally honest, I don't know what to make of it and can't be sure she does either. Although there's this invented language in the poems, it reminds you how incantatory and arcane poetry can be. I enjoy the sound of it, it's cool for sure."

"*Cool.* See, that's exactly it, cool," said Lily. "The reason I ask is this: she's a very stylish girl, she's got style in everything she does, and she's clever — not brilliant, but extremely clever. What I mean is, I'd be surprised if she truly had any compassionate or insightful things to say, through art, about this life, this life thing we're all submerged in! I love her, I do, but I just don't know if she is capable of creating anything really vital."

Do you know who is a real artist? Your mother. I make drawings and write stories, my parents are painters and printmakers, my grandparents, too; their paintings and prints are framed and hanging on the walls in the Virginia house. But your mother is a person who is an artist in all she does. Not in grand gestures, rather, with subtlety. And like all true artists, she's equipped with a finely calibrated bullshit detector, has an eye capable of recognizing the sacred in the profane, seeing the beauty of common things, discerning a light, however faint, germinating in the rot and shadow. *She shows you where to look between the garbage and the flowers,* sang Leonard Cohen.

It's also worth noting that she possesses the hand of a

technically accomplished limner as well. The oil portraits and the graphite still lifes she produced in high school are displayed back in her family's home in Waterloo. The work is far superior to any of the trash my brother Lyman and I ever produced at that age while we hustled for awards and fussed over our portfolios for Cooper and RISD.

After her accident, we spent most of our days nesting in the big beautiful house of my mentor, cooking, reading, and making art together. I was at the desk in the master bedroom writing an article on wild mushrooms for the paper while she sat propped-up in bed, working on the illustration for the piece, left handed. I got up to put on some hot water and took a look: the fringed edges of the caps and the lines of the gills were delicately, if shakily, rendered. Executed with her non-dominant hand, it was turning out beautiful.

I returned to the desk.

"Don't move," she said to me.

She'd set down the drawing of fungus, and started a drawing of me.

After she left I discovered a canvas bag full of pens and papers, receipts, fortunes from fortune cookies, fossils, acorns, charred nubs of palo santo — things we'd accumulated during our summer together in that house. I threw most of it out except for a stack of her drawings. I was surprised to find several other portraits I didn't know she'd drawn. Some were of my head in profile, some with my head bowed, while I was reading perhaps. A few were of just my lips and nose. One drawn from a low perspective shows my eyes closed, my shoulders bare, my hands curled at my chin. She captured me asleep. Looking at these drawings, seeing my body transfigured through her eye and careful hand, I recalled what I'd heard James Turrell talk of at a lecture in Ithaca — the sensation of being painted in light with light.

About two months after you were aborted, we were invited to contribute pieces to a group show at a friend's gallery. I drew a wizard with a tangled beard and a third-eye sprouting from the folds of skin below his wizard's cap. That wizard was emblematic of my artistic ambitions in those somber days: I drew things that I felt would lift her spirits: fungi and sabertooth tiger skulls, inside jokes about wookies and warlocks and witches. I even drew a cartoon of her riding a sandworm on the planet Arrakis.

The night before the show's opening there was a lunar eclipse, a full Corn Moon that also happened to be a blood moon. I biked over to her place to ask her if she wanted to go for a walk in the prairie and see the moon. She was in bed working on her submission. She'd been working on it in secret.

"What do you think? Isn't it cute?" she asked.

Mounted on her drawing board was a black and white landscape of webbed branches and woven leaves, the wrinkled caps of morels fruiting in a carpet of creeping mosses. The bower of flora and fungi surrounded a dark cavity, a black womb; nested at the center of the composition was a fetal skeleton, its bulbous skull bent, its tiny hands folded up, as if sleeping.

Blood Moon

(ENCHANTMENT)

Sry I've been acting weird / distant.

Is not fair to you.

Venus is in retrograde.

Come over?

NINE

"Some say cavalry and others claim infantry or a fleet of long oars is
the supreme sight on the black earth. I say it is the one you love.
And I would rather see her supple step and motion of light on her face
than chariots of the Lydians or ranks of foot soldiers in bronze."

—SAPPHO

T HE NIGHT SHE TOLD ME she was leaving, she'd made stir fry and lit candles around her apartment.

"I was waiting for my feelings to come back," she said. "It was a universal truth when it was, and then it wasn't. I'm sorry."

"I've managed to love you more than I thought I could love anybody," I said.

"I know. I always knew."

"How?"

"The way you look at me," she said. "I'm so sorry."

I had nothing else worth saying. What I'd feared for months had been made clear: she had nothing left to give to our relationship, nothing left for me. Whatever she needed to do now, she needed to do it alone. I got up to leave.

"Tie your shoe," she said.

That morning I'd received a book in the mail from my friend Johanna. It was a copy of Elizabeth McCracken's memoir about her stillborn child, *An Exact Replica of a Figment of My Imagination.* I read it completely in one sitting. I was emboldened by the fact that, even in the face of such a loss, the author and her partner stayed together. My spirits were raised to such a degree that I wrote, like really wrote, for the first time in months. On a bench overlooking the railroad tracks that receded south in a tunnel of yellow trees, I wrote page after page, letter after letter, to the kid, our kid that never lived.

"You're going to be okay, I know it," was the last thing she said that night.

I pedaled through her lawn, frightening the rabbits from their hiding places in the grass and setting the neighbor's dog into a barking fit for maybe the last time.

I didn't go home. I biked on, pedaling in loops through town, past Clark's Buffet, past St. Mary's. Moans and shouts tore from my lips, I couldn't control it. My teeth were chattering, I felt dizzy. I dismounted and walked my bike and started to dry heave in an alley.

Nobody noticed or seemed to care that I was doubled over on the ground. People passed me on the sidewalk, some of them in masks, others with capes and wigs. They were kids, they were all drunk; it was Halloween night.

A friend from school saw me in the crowd and yelled to me from across the street.

"Are you okay?"

I didn't respond. She crossed the street and stood over me.

"Need me to call someone?"

I told her I was fine, and convinced her I wasn't wasted. She said I should come with her to the bar, a bunch of our other classmates were inside. As I followed down the stairs I knew I was making a mistake. That basement pub was the place where a local poet nearly drank himself to death the year before, after his sister was killed in a head-on collision while driving back east after visiting him in Iowa.

"This landscape is cursed, do you know that? The natives knew it, and the Mormons found out, too," I said to the first-year fiction writer who offered to buy me a drink.

He looked into his pint glass and sipped slowly.

"Surf fucking ballroom. Big Bopper, Richie Valens, Buddy Holly! Those poor motherfuckers didn't make it out of Iowa alive.

And you know what? I won't either. I'll die here on the prairie. I actually want to," I said.

Ronny, my closest friend from school, overheard me. He asked if I needed to talk.

"I should go," I said.

"Okay. You need a ride?" he asked.

"Actually, is it cool if I sleep on your couch?"

I couldn't sleep. I'd never felt so exhausted, my mind spun and my body ached. I tried to make myself vomit but couldn't; there wasn't anything left to puke up. I could hear the rhythmic thrumming of Ronny and his girlfriend's sleeping breaths, the drone of the fridge. I switched positions on the couch, then moved to the chair and then back to the couch, turned my pillow over again. The urge to scream would bubble up, and it was everything I could do not to let it escape and startle my hosts. In the darkness I counted ceiling panels, the fronds of the hanging fern, the books on the shelf.

Vonnegut once wrote a letter to his buddy who was moving to Iowa, urging his friend to go watch a Hawkeyes game at Kinnick Stadium. It wouldn't have taken much convincing for me; as soon as I arrived in Iowa I had purchased football tickets. Back east nobody in my friend group of artists, musicians, and outdoorsy-types shared my pleasure for watching college basketball at the bar or listening to the Giants on the radio. I took Ed, Sun, and Zeus to the Cornell-Harvard hockey match our sophomore year, but after the first period, they decided they'd seen enough.

"At least I can say I went to a 'sporting game' before I graduated," said Ed and laughed.

"Yeah, a social experiment for sure," said Sun.

Zeus nodded and packed a bowl as we walked through the snow-plowed parking lot.

When I lived in Bushwick, the folks at Roberta's pizzeria initially thought I only watched the Giants to be ironic. But I showed up every Sunday for two years and watched the games on their television set above the bar in the garden. Over the course of those seasons, a good number of the Roberta's staff joined me around that little screen, swigging Bud, rooting for the Giants, and we became one tribe.

And who knows why, but I kept this sports-loving part of myself hidden from her and most of my friends in Iowa. I was one of only a handful of writers to get season tickets to the Hawkeyes. The Hawks kept their beaks slightly above water the first two seasons, going

8–5 and 7–6 respectively. But this year they were quietly putting together a miracle season. On the night she left me, the Hawks were an improbable 7–0.

"Season opener," I said to myself, counting ceiling tiles from Ronny's couch. "Home, versus the Illinois State Redbirds. Division 1-AA, a decent team nonetheless. Hawks won 31–14. Illinois State only scored in the fourth, garbage time. The Hawks had their third stringers in . . ."

That's what I'd do: if I couldn't sleep I'd fix my mind on the Hawks, run through each game of the season in my head, each period, each down if I had to.

Game two: in-state rivalry. Hawks pounded the Cyclones in Ames. The media was all over Trump and Cruz in the crowd. The Hawks proved they were a second half team. Final score, 31–17.

Next was a night game; Iowa downed Pitt in a true nailbiter. The kicker, a local kid, drilled a 57-yarder as time expired. Hawks by a field goal, 27–24.

Iowa embarrassed North Texas, 62–12.

The defense came up big in the next game, when the Hawks stuffed a ranked Wisconsin squad 10–6, at Camp Randall.

Game six was homecoming. Illinois. I went to the game by myself. Wes Lunt shot holes in Hawks' secondary, but still hung on to win it, 29–20.

The Hawks came through for me that night on Ronny's couch. The birds starting singing, the sky was purpling and nearing dawn, and I was knocked out and sleeping at last.

Bee Balm

(PORTRAIT OF A COUPLE IN WILDFLOWERS

AS TWO SEPARATE PEOPLE)

Caryatids carved

In our likenesses saved

The roof from falling

In on itself

Left on a shelf they'll survive

Us; But the wind is blowing and I long to be

My shadow of me in the flowers.

Dear Catalpa,

Ingrid said, "Statistically speaking, couples usually don't make it through these sort of things."

She's been a good friend to me, and her statement may be a valid one, but I still resented her for saying it.

"Do you know what you should really be doing? You should try making art," she said. That was two days after we broke up; I could barely make oatmeal.

Ingrid later texted, "Hope the ice begins to melt. Hope the clouds part soon!" with a bunch of emojis. The message, her love and concern, her desire to console, touched me. But why hope for the inevitable healing processes to do their inevitable thing? Fractured bones mend with or without our well-wishing. Praying winter will end is pointless; winters end all on their own. Still, I was praying I could carry the weight of each day, praying I'd make it until spring. I was watching the Hawks and praying for the Hail Mary pass. I was praying the feeling back into the woman I love.

Golden Eagle

(AQUILA CHRYSAETOS)

SON: *How did you and mom know?*

FATHER: *We didn't think about it that way.*

SON: *You got married after five days?*

FATHER: *Yes, in Mexico.*

SON: *That just seems kind of insane.*

FATHER: *If I'd waited until the timing seemed right to reenlist, have children, marry your mother, I'd still be waiting. Being ready only gets you so far; doing the thing itself is what shows you the way.*

TEN

DUDE, YOU'RE IN THE SAME hotel Robin Williams checked into when he hung himself," said Ed.

I was in a towel, the phone was on speaker on the dresser. I parted the blinds of my window and watched the churning confluence of the Des Moines and Raccoon rivers, the Des Moines skyline, the mustering herds of cumulus clouds, all of it painted dishwater gray.

"*Hanged* himself," I said. "And thank you."

"I'm fucking with you. I know now is not the best time, I'm sorry. I love you buddy," said Ed. "This residency is going to be good for you. Come on dude, Robin Williams killed himself at home in California."

A week after she left, I left for a residency hosted by a design firm in Des Moines. I didn't apply for it or know why they chose me; perhaps someone in my program nominated me. Anyway, the timing was good. The other fellows I met seemed better suited for the residency — planners, architects, engineers, and MBAs. I wasn't quite sure what I was doing there, but honestly didn't care to know, either.

"Wowie zowie!" said Dot. "You're the writer! Your job may very well be the most important one of all." As one of the firm's partners, Dot had been assigned to oversee the fellows. "The writer is our wizard! The writer is responsible for conjuring up the whole narrative for this project. We're just so lucky to have you, a writer, on board."

Dot and the design firm would have been better off with a necromancer instead of a wizard for the project at hand. It involved redeveloping a concrete clot of parking garages and vacant high rises currently situated between the new conference hotel being contracted by the firm hosting the residency and the existing conference center. Urban renewal wasn't my wheelhouse, artistically or ethically, but digging into a creative project, no matter what the flavor, felt like a much needed distraction. "A busy bee avoids sorrow," she used to tell me.

Des Moines wasn't so bad. It kind of looked like an actual city. It was certainly more city-like than Cedar Rapids. The contemporary art museum, I was told, was first-rate. Not to mention the botanical center. They seemed proud of their four square blocks of a bohemian district, with its requisite overpriced antique stores, overpriced sandwich shops, and overpriced cocktail bars. One of the firm's architects proclaimed that while attending a food truck festival at one of the downtown's mixed use art spaces, she waited a full hour for a kimchi taco and a cup of lobster mac and cheese.

"There were lines! It was awesome!" she said.

Okay, so Des Moines sucked. But on the bright side, I had three square meals a day and a clean place for a week (with a pool, no less) that was not Iowa City. And I had a little scratch in the bank thanks to the firm. Most importantly, though, I found I could make art again, write again, after so many months. I felt if anything would get me through, it would be my art.

And God, was I writing. Non-stop at night in my hotel room, filling whole graph paper notebooks, writing until my pens dried out, though none of it was for the residency project.

I managed an hour or two of sleep each night before reporting to the office at 7:30 for the morning briefing. Though the other fellows seemed especially enthused by the never-ending meetings and presentations, none of it made any sense to me at all, and I found myself locked in my mind, worrying about her. I journaled through video conferences with city planners from Nashville and Portland, drew during PowerPoint presentations given by a meteorologist and pitches delivered by local developers. On a hard-hat tour of the project site, one of the fellows inquired about an ornate pagoda, which sprouted like a lone morel on the banks of the Des Moines River.

"Ah-ha!" said Dot. "That's a gift from our sister city Shijiazhuang in China. Shi, jia, zhuang? Right, Shijiazhuang? That's how you pronounce it, I'm sure of it, I've been there. It's our sister city, after all."

She directed her nervous monologue at the Chinese-American landscape architect from Wisconsin, who simply shrugged.

Beyond the pagoda was a bridge that had been tagged with the words, "HEAL WHAT IS BROKEN," in scripted white letters. Jotting down that message was the first note I'd taken that could be, in some way, interpreted as having anything to do with the project.

"I want to get my hands on that," said Dot, jutting her finger in the direction of my notebook.

I turned the notebook over, concealing it against my thigh.

"I guess you'll just have to wait and see," I said.

"Oh, I literally cannot wait to see what our writer has been up to!" said Dot.

And what had their writer been up to? Well, he'd passed up joining the other fellows at the bar the night before. He kept his phone off all day, took his meals alone in one of the empty conference rooms. He wrote lists in Sharpie on his hands and arms that said things like, *1. Acknowledge / observe anxious / fear-based thoughts; 2. Let worries GO!; 3. Stay focused on the PRESENT; 4. GO TO BOTANICAL CENTER; 5. Get tea for her.*

"I'm going for a walk," I said. "I need to hone this whole narrative a little bit, in private."

All of the other residents were buzzing around the office, scanning and flipping through aerial maps, squinting at screens with data on gray water retention and the albedo levels of parking garage roofs. Only Dot heard what I said.

"Who am I to interfere with the magic of the writing process?" asked Dot, flashing me a big smile. "Ernest Hemingway had funny little habits himself, didn't he? Like, I read that he worked at his typewriter standing up."

"He blew his brains out," I said. "I can tell you that much, for sure. Adiós, Dot!"

It was windy. I crossed the cement bridge that spanned the river and ascended the hill to the tea shop, her favorite tea shop.

She went to Des Moines without me one Sunday to buy loose tea and visit the botanical center. I tried not to act hurt when she returned and sat with me on the sofa and showed me the pictures she'd taken of lilies and cycads, bonsais and pitcher plants.

"Gong-Fu, the tea shop, was closed for some reason! Fuck my life," she said.

The two of us would visit Des Moines some weekend soon, she said. She'd show me the dankest banh-mi spot, we'd go to the botanical center, and then the contemporary art center. This plan for a trip, however abstract, infused me with a reassuring calm; maybe because it was a sketch of a future with us together when everything else, day-to-day, seemed so bleak.

I was driving the guy behind the counter at Gong-Fu crazy. He was annoyed as I nosed through their catalog and sent him off to fetch different varieties of teas for me to try.

"Camel's Breath," I said. "And the Golden Tuo Cha, could you bring me that, too? Also the Bai Mudan, bring that."

In my hotel room, I wrote a description of each tea and its brewing instructions on a piece of graph paper. I included factoids like, "*tuo cha* means bird's nest," with drawings of cartoon insects and birds and fungi. I sealed it all — notes, drawings, teas — in an envelope I'd snagged from the firm's supply room. I printed her name and address in big letters, and pasted the package with more than enough postage. But I decided to hold off on sending it. I wanted to see how I felt about mailing it once the end of the week arrived.

"We've got big dreams. I mean, we're the insurance capital of the country," said one of the firm's planners at the morning meeting.

"Actually, that distinction belongs to Hartford," said Dot. "We're technically the number two insurance city. But still, we're big time."

"Right, right," said the planner. "But we can dream bigger. We want to be the next Omaha, the next Kansas City, even."

"I'm sorry to hear that," I said.

Everyone at the table swiveled in their Aeron chairs to face me, their eyes sockets dilated, like a congress of owls. I'd been silent up until that point.

"That just seems like a bleak aspiration," I said. "Not to be a dick, of course."

No one at the table knew what to make of my comment, and I wasn't totally sure what I meant by it, or why I'd said it, either. But Dot was squinting and nodding at me. She seemed to be grooving with what I was laying down. Thank God for Dot. I went on.

"Des Moines isn't in the mountains or on the water. It's a city surrounded by farms, sort of like an agrarian metropolis, which is pretty sick, I think. Those parking garages could be urban farms, the skywalks could be converted into hydroponic greenhouses."

"Why not raise chickens and bees in the city?" I continued. One of the partners pulled the cap off his pen and began jotting down notes. "Other pollinators, too, like butterflies. We could have goats. That would be really cool, right? The goats of Des Moines?"

I was speaking off the cuff and out my ass, but I couldn't stop.

"Someday, somebody in Los Angeles or Brooklyn will be eating brunch on the rooftop garden of some locavore joint," I said. "They'll be scooping ketchup made from that restaurant's tomatoes, grown in that restaurant's rooftop hothouse, and they'll be smearing that ketchup on eggs, eggs that were laid just down the block by the chickens of that restaurant's sister establishment. And that person will look to their companion and be like, 'Oh damn, you know what? I feel like I'm in Des Moines right now.'"

And more or less, that was the narrative I ended up penning for the project. They ate that shit right up, took that rambling, half-baked urban farm pitch and ran. The other fellows spent the next two days rendering hop trellises in parking spots, monarch flyways on top of the YMCA, vertical flower beds and hoop houses in the vacant lots. "The Farm District Plan" was pitched to the public on Friday, and I served as the keynote.

"Take it from me," I said to the room of city council members and developers. "I'm from New York City. I know what it looks like to have Mother Nature on the run. I know what the sight of a single crocus quivering through a rupture in the asphalt can do for a soul brutalized by the cement and glass of the urban landscape. I have big dreams for Des Moines, but they aren't too big," I paced the room. "I have this dream of a man picking wildflowers in a parking lot turned endemic prairie, right here, downtown. I see him biking those flowers home to the woman he loves, pregnant and wrapped in a saree, singing Patsy Cline to herself in the kitchen. I don't know, maybe she's got a lemon tart in the oven."

"We put out a call for a writer, but I didn't think we'd land ourselves Whitman!" said Dot.

The other fellows and planners laughed. We were all gathered at an arcade bar following the final presentation.

"I just knew you'd come through!" said Dot.

Back at the hotel, I turned my phone on, but even after four days, no one had attempted to contact me — most significantly, not her. I decided then to buy a ticket for a flight to Arizona, where Sun and Johanna were living.

"My flight arrives in Phoenix at tomorrow," I said to Sun.

"Awesome. Stay as long as you need. The desert is a real healing place. You'll see," said Sun.

I rolled up my shirts and socks on the bed, stacked my hats, and stuffed them into my duffle on top of the package I hadn't mailed to her.

Patsy Cline

("SWEET DREAMS")

Sweet dreams of you
Things I know can't come true
Why can't I forget the past
Start loving someone new
Instead of having sweet
Dreams about you?

Dear Catalpa,

I encountered one of my favorite poems at a Quaker Meeting, years ago, at the Brooklyn Friends Meeting off the Hoyt-Schermerhorn stop. It had been a quiet worship, only a few messages, but forty minutes in one of the Friends, a tall old man with a white ponytail, sprang up from his pew and began to dance. He bounded around the meeting house, astonishingly agile and nimble-footed for his age and frame. Half Salome, half Ichabod Crane, he dipped and lurched, shimmied and swayed through the sun-filled sanctuary. Just as abruptly as the performance began, it ended; he took his seat, closed his eyes, and bowed his head in quiet contemplation. It was announced at the following meeting that just a few days after that, his wife discovered him flat on his back in their vegetable garden in Red Hook. Please look up this poet in the afterlife. Tell him you're my kid; there's a chance he remembers me.

Over the past five years, I've spent many hours in worship.

I've sat with the Quakers and sang in black Pentecostal churches in Bed-Stuy, received ashes on the first day of Lent and lit yizkor candles on the high holidays. I've done yoga at a Sikh ashram high in the New Mexico desert and slept in bunks in dorm rooms with monks. I've read the *Bhagavad Gita* by the light of a juniper campfire and had my seven chakras cleansed to the drone of an electronic tambura.

One may say, "Plenty of people find God after they've hit the mat. His hair fell out, she left him after some heavy shit, so he cracked up and started talking to God." And to that I say that's about the long and short of it. You're not in love until you are, you don't want to die until you feel like you already have, and you don't know the Divine until you see its hand in all things.

It wouldn't be fair to call me an atheist before I found faith, since I mostly identified as an anti-theist. Despite my upbringing, or maybe because of it, I spent the first quarter century of my life believing religion wasn't a force of goodwill or compassion, as it often masqueraded. I felt the different flavors of Abrahamic faiths and eastern religions, agnosticisms and spiritualities, were essentially one heap of divisive, inhumane, and fear-based institutions serving as superstitious roadblocks, obstructions in recognizing the inalienable and equivalent worth of each member of our species living for this brief moment on this wet planet spinning in space.

Your grandfather comes from a line of Sephardic Jews, punted off the toe of the Italian boot and landing in Flatbush. Due to the staunch faith of his Neapolitan mother, he was raised devoutly Catholic. Your grandmother is bred of a handsome yet dower Nordic stock, humorless Lutherans of the frigid middle west (a genealogy not unlike that of your mother). Your grandmother, however, converted to Catholicism while our family lived in Italy. As a result I attended Catholic Schools in the states, served as an altar boy alongside your uncle Lyman, and not once did I feel any stirring of anything that resembled belief. For many years, the lone religious experience I could cite occured on the eve of my confirmation, at a retreat house on some nameless lake in the Catskills, when I got my first blowjob from a shy horsey-looking girl I hadn't spoken to until that weekend.

Whether I was in some college slum in Ithaca, a stark room of crumbling plaster in an old Roman palazzo, or a Bushwick loft / bedbug ranch, I'd receive postcards from your grandmother telling me I was in her prayers. On the reverse of these antique postcards depicting the Arches National park or the Mermaids of Weeki Wachee would be your grandmother's neat script explaining how she'd been lighting candles, seeing psychics on my behalf, and saying prayers for me to St. Monica, mother of Augustine and patron of all moms wishing faith upon their kids. I keep these postcards in spite of the sentiment. But then one summer day, and I can't really say how, your grandmother's prayers were answered.

I was in upstate New York, the Sunday before Labor Day, the year all of my hair fell out. I asked your Aunt Ruth if she'd drive me out to the Friends Meeting in Perry City. Perry City was a city only in name, since it was actually a lakeside hamlet of two hundred residents at best, perched in the woods between Ithaca and Trumansburg. Ruth stayed in the car, smoking and listening to the radio. I climbed through coneflowers, milkweed, and spotted Joe Pye weed growing along the path that led to the meeting house. The whole mass of vetch and bloom crowded out the slate sidewalk that led to the yellow meeting house, a Scandinavian clapboard structure with a steeply gabled tin roof sitting at the edge of a dense woods.

I shrunk into one of the seats closest to the wall and watched the movements of each Friend as they entered, hoping to take a cue from one of them. Several months with Emerson and George Fox's *Book of Miracles* on my nightstand had landed me there, but I had few, if any, expectations when it came to the actual service. Some Friends bowed with their chins to their chests, others lay their hands on their laps. Most closed their eyes.

Unconsciously, I removed my cap. I'd only recently been diagnosed with alopecia universalis, and this may have been the first time I'd revealed my hairless head in the company of strangers. I closed my eyes and attempted to let my thoughts drift off untethered, objective and shapeless as smoke. As to-do lists and daily routines threatened to distract me, I inhaled through my nose, and let them go with each exhale. Before long, and at my very first meeting no less, a vision came.

There was a stage with red velvet curtains drawn by gold cords, like the one at my elementary school. Under the spotlight was a conical pile, a volcano-like structure of rags and carpets clotted with hair and gravel, cigarette-burned rugs, stuffed animals, and every kind of textile scrap and garment. The pile shuddered with the tremblings of a hatching egg, or a butterfly twitching from its chrysalis. Buried inside that Mike Kelley-like assemblage was my own naked body. I watched myself wrestle to push free. I flung hairy sweaters and itchy scarves from my face and chest. I coughed and gagged, dislodging lint wads from my nose and mouth, rubbed the dust and grit from my eyes.

"It's an interesting detail," Johanna said later when I described the vision to her. "That mention of the dust in the eyes especially. And an auspicious vision to receive in upstate New York, land of the Six Nations."

She explained how Hiawatha and the Great Peacemaker had brought healing to the wicked sachem Todahaho by touching his body, a body contorted and deformed by hatred. Hiawatha instructed the sachem to lay his head in his lap as he whispered soothing words to him and combed the poisonous snakes from his hair.

"With his fingers, Hiawatha cleaned Todahaho's ears and said, 'The dust of death was in your ears, you could not hear,'" said Johanna. "He then cleared the sachem's mouth and said, 'The dust of death was in your mouth, you could not speak.' And finally, he rubbed the sachem's eyes and said, 'The dust of death is in your eyes, how can you see?' That was dust of death in your vision, and it was on you."

I've only ever received a handful of visions since that first meeting. I can recall one involving a memory from a century bike ride on Long Island. I'm floating on my back, with each hand I'm locking fingers with my mother and father. My parents are in turn holding the hands of my siblings who are linked in a chain of people extending across the water — people I've cared for or who have cared for me: old students, ex-girlfriends, coworkers, relatives, the living and the dead all floating there with me in the waters off Orient Point. I've received other beautiful visions as well.

But now every time I go to Meeting and when I meditate at home, this recurring vision comes to me. The first time it came to me I heard the chorus of my fellow Friends' breaths, the siren of an emergency vehicle on the street, the beeping of a backing up truck, bells of neighboring churches, one tolling Beethoven's "Ode to Joy." And then, even though it was a snowy December morning, there came the oceanic sound of wind sifting through the leaves of a deep green woods at night.

In this vision, the full moon of May, the Flower Moon, is shining. We have hatched a plan for a full moon walk through the meadow and the woods. When I arrive, I see her keeping watch, wrapped in a green saree at the kitchen window. There's always something in the oven in these visions — a lemon tart, a quiche — and we sway over the kitchen tile to the Byrds or else the Blue Sky Boys.

"We should get going," she says.

"I forgot my headlamp," I say.

"That's okay, we won't need it," she says.

Where the woods peel off to give way to the meadow, the moon is shining bright. But under the thick canopy of trees along the trails, the moonlight is snuffed out in an inked darkness.

"Step up," she says. "This way."

She takes me by the hands. "Watch your head. Careful, there's a root there." She leads me through the labyrinthine wooded trails.

"Puddle."

My eyes never adjust to the dark, but she guides me through the night. She's run these trails for years, and the way is as familiar and innate to her as the melodies of songs one learns as a kid. As the tree cover begins to recede, the moonlight touches on a garland of dried chrysanthemums hanging from a bush.

"Whoa!" I say.

The trail opens on another meadow where a mansion flexes in the moonlight, lit up like a circus tent. The lights are on in every window and the silhouettes of bodies pass between the rooms.

"What?" she asks. "Oh that," she says, noticing the house. "Isn't it awful? We'll never live in a place like that."

She hadn't noticed the mansion because her eyes had been closed. They'd been closed while she led me through the woods, they'd been closed the whole time.

"Have you seen the Black Angel?" she asks.

"No," I say.

"Well I'm taking you there," she says.

And that's where it ends.

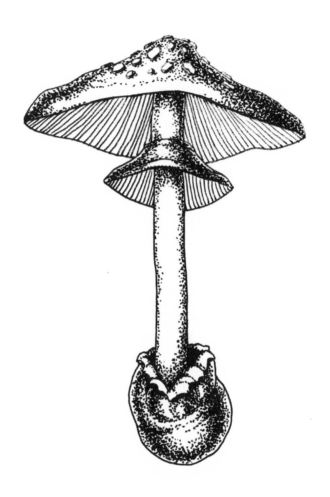

Black Angel

(RODINA FELDEVERT)

"To lose someone: we suffer because the departed, the absent, has become something imaginary and unreal. But our desire for him is not imaginary." —Simone Weil

Dear Catalpa,

"Nothing can make up for the absence of someone whom we love, and it would be wrong to try to find a substitute, we must simply hold out and see it through. That sounds very hard at first, but at the same time it is a great consolation, for the gap, as long as it remains unfulfilled, preserves the bonds between us. It is nonsense to say that God fills the gap. God doesn't fill it, but on the contrary keeps it empty and so helps us to keep alive our former communion with each other, even at the cost of pain." —*Dietrich Bonhoeffer*

Nerine

On a good day
you remember it
wrong: give your heart
to no one not even
an animal.

Dear Catalpa,

Kindertotenlieder, or *Songs on the Death of Children* is the title of a collection of nearly four hundred poems written by Rückert as a means to write his way out from under the garment of grief following the death of his kids. His critics disregarded the work, calling it a manic attempt of poetic resuscitation. But Gustav Mahler was so moved by Rückert's poems that he composed a song cycle of the same name inspired by them. His wife, Alma, thought it inauspicious for her husband to create music pertaining to such a subject, and begged Gustav to abandon the project. He didn't, and the work was a hit in Vienna. Alma became pregnant that same year, and their child, a daughter, died in infancy. I don't know if it's true, but I read somewhere that Alma became depressed and left Mahler. In her absence, he slid into a breakdown, showing up at high profile parties and bourgeoisie functions around Ringstrasse, Vienna a total mess. And in spite of the fact that she was gone, he introduced everyone to his wife: a wax mannequin in the likeness of Alma. He dressed the mannequin in her clothes and draped it with her jewelry. He dragged it up marble stairs and down carpeted halls, through the cobblestoned streets of the city by its limp doll's arm.

It's the winter solstice, the darkest day. I'm at my parent's house watching *The Godfather* marathon. During the first film I was shaken by a scene between Don Corleone and Bonasera the coroner.

"Well, my friend," says the Don. "Are you ready to do me this service?"

And Bonasera, nervous as hell, says, "Yes, what do you want me to do?"

The two men walk into the embalming room. On the table is a shrouded corpse.

"I want you to use all of your powers, and all of your skills," says Don Corleone. "I don't want his mother to see him this way."

He draws back the sheet to reveal a blood-soaked body, the body of his own son, Sonny.

"Look," says Don Corleone, choking back tears. "Look how they massacred my boy."

Lately, I feel like two men: the grief-stricken Don, and the trembling coroner. I've summoned myself to use all of my powers, all of my skills, to transform something horrible into a thing of beauty for her.

Art is the accomplice of love.

Saguaro

I dreamed we were doing karaoke at the American Legion on Muscatine, but it was simultaneously the Roadhouse from Twin Peaks. You chose this Sons of the Pioneers song and the DJ didn't think he had it, but it turned out he did. Instead of singing we just let the tune play and watched the lyrics projected on the wall. Every beating heart beats a rhythm that is blue, and the moon has cast a blue reflection in the dew. So the wind while on its way seems to cry and sigh and say, blue, blue prairie. *The crowd was really into it; maybe they thought it was some sort of performance art. They clapped and whistled.*

I said, "I'm sorry I'm still in love with you," and you said, "I'm not."

ELEVEN

HE MISSION SAN XAVIER DEL BAC was founded
in 1692 by the Italian Padre Eusebio Kino, but this
structure we're standing in today only dates to 1780.
The original was destroyed by Apaches," said the docent.

I wasn't on their tour, but I'd been eavesdropping on this geri-
atric flock of snowbirds shuffling through the sooty nave, cough-
ing and asking seemingly rhetorical questions at the shrines and
architectural curiosities along the way. The mission, the White
Dove of the Desert, was an alabaster oasis hovering on the Sonoran
horizon. Once inside, Sun, Johanna, and I were blown away by its
superb tackiness, the grotesqueness of the little icons and statues.
The Christ was too veiny and attenuated; there was just too much
blood spilling from his thorny crown, pouring in torrents down
his skeletal head. If Caravaggio was commissioned to paint the
sacred images in San Luigi dei Francese in Rome, then it seemed
like R. Crumb or Howard Finster could have produced the holy

works in the White Dove on the Tohono O'odham reservation south of Tucson.

"Who's she?" asked a man with a silver eagle bolo and Korean War veteran's cap. He was pointing to a carved wood statue of some saint, a woman with praying hands and braided hair, fringed buckskin dress.

"Saint Kateri Tekakwitha, Lily of the Mohawks," said the docent. "I guess the church needed a wooden Indian."

The group laughed. A couple snapped some photos of the statue with their phones before moving on with the group.

I exited through the heavy mesquite doors and found Sun and Johanna in the courtyard taking pictures of a headless, handless statue of an unknown saint.

"Pretty sick, huh?" said Sun. "Did you hear that bit about the lions?"

There were two wooden lions flanking the altar. Like the mission itself, the lions weren't the originals. The originals had been stolen by one of the church custodians, a deaf man who'd grown up on the res. He'd schlepped the lions into the desert at night, axed them to pieces, and burned them to ash as the sun came up. When they questioned the custodian, he didn't deny it. He signed to them that the Lord had compelled him to destroy the lions since they'd been possessed by evil spirits. And for some reason, this story, like nearly everything else, is something I want to share with her.

The idea of a gift store in a place of worship seems profane, but I followed my friends in anyhow. The shop was chock-full of chintzy dreamcatchers and wildlife print t-shirts, plastic statues of Our Lady of Guadalupe and White Dove keychains. They had these little snow globes with saguaros and roadrunners in them. There were some corny postcards on a postcard rack; I grabbed the best one.

"We used to catch those on the playground!" said Johanna. I held a card with a horned lizard wearing sunglasses and a backwards hat.

"Horned lizards or horned toads?" I asked.

"Same thing," she said. "Though it's a reptile, not an amphibian. When they're frightened they shoot blood from their eyes!"

Driving through the res on our way back to Tucson, I hung my head out the window and let the dry air blow over my head. A chain-link enclosure surrounded what looked like a huge garden rising up from the sand beside a trailer park. The rows of sugary-colored blossoms turned out to be silken bows and fake flowers, all hanging from the stalks of skinny white crosses.

"Dias de los Muertos," said Johanna. "The parade is Sunday."

"Oh yeah. Biggest one in the country," said Sun.

"If you don't mind me saying so, why not take the intention of the abortion to the parade?" said Johanna. "My friends Ben and Emily marched last year in the memory of their pitbull."

"Or we don't have to go at all," said Sun.

"No, I want to go," I said.

In the morning we hiked into the mountains beyond Gates Pass and I fell for the saguaros. The first thing that struck me about them was how comical yet majestic they appeared, how anthropomorphic, with their green arms stuck up in a pose of surrender or worship. They dotted the craggy landscape in legions, each cactus the survivor of thousands of days of thirst and kiln-like heat, freezing desert nights and vandalism by woodpeckers. Each had waited faithfully sixty years before its first flower bloomed, a vigilant hundred until its first limb. The hairy scorpions and gambel quails, barrel cacti and diamondback rattlers, everything was girded by the forces of survival; all Sonoran lifeforms possessed the same stubborn imperative to endure, to persist in spite of a world bent on burying them in the sand. Twenty of the twenty-one creosote bushes at the epicenter of an atomic bomb site across the border in New Mexico sprouted forth green leaves a decade after the explosion. If you left you sandals out on the porch, they'd be devoured by the javelinas.

"Be careful of those chollas," said Sun, ambling ahead of me on the path.

"They're fighters," I said.

"They'll fuck you up," said Sun.

"I like them," I said. "Hey, we should go to the Grand Canyon this week. Can we do that?"

"Yeah, man," said Sun. "I've been meaning to hit it up, we can do Sedona on the way. We can get our auras read."

I overtook him on the path, scrambled up to an overlook point.

"And we should get matching tattoos," I said. "I want to get a cactus flower. It's about fucking time we got the same tattoo."

"Of course, man, flowers are cool," said Sun. "You know I'm down for that."

TWELVE

I<small>T WAS A DESERT NIGHT</small>, and cold. We parked downtown and followed the crowds dressed for The Day of the Dead. Women's faces were painted to resemble skulls, babies in strollers were dressed as skeletons, dogs wore skeleton sweaters. People surged through the streets and sidewalks toward the parade. Heavy bass and hip hop drum beats, funk horns and traditional Mexican guitars reached us blocks before the parade came into view. A skeleton prom queen popped and locked with her parasol on her shoulder. She wore tall platforms and danced precariously atop a painted skull float.

"It's like she's a dead Cinderella and her pumpkin is like a skull stagecoach," said Sun.

"Yeah," I said. He was more stoned than I thought.

Two men operating a papier mâché zombie Bernie Sanders puppet pushed past us. Sun was scanning the congested sidewalk looking for a good view when I shoved ahead into the parade's guts and marched with it. He caught up to me as we fell in behind a troop of skeleton bagpipers in tam o'shanters caps and kilts.

There were people dancing and beating drums, jugglers juggling flaming batons and stilt walkers, old men on unicycles, dead mimes. A woman to our left wore a massive skeletal mermaid apparatus on her shoulders, a woman beside her wore two additional pairs of bone arms like a boney Hindu goddess. Chicano Catholics held posters with pictures of their departed loved-ones. A padre in a hooded sweatshirt and an Arizona Wildcats cap rattled off the names of his departed parishioners through a megaphone. A woman in a wheelchair pushed by a teenage boy held a box on her lap decorated with flowers and twinkling LED lights. Inside was a photograph of a young man in a football uniform, below was the word HIJO.

The parade squeezed through an underpass and re-emerged into the chill night. A woman walked alone with red and black carnations in her hair. She reminded me of her: same posture and gait, long dark hair like hers. Concealed beneath her black lace shawl, her arm was bundled in a sling.

"I wish she was here," I said. "I wish she could see all this."

My friend took my hand in his and we marched on in the parade, swallowed by the cries of bagpipes and horns and mariachis.

Creosote

Where I learn
To surrender owls
Whistle nobody
Knows the trouble

I've seen cactus
Flowers bloom
Under full moons
Knowing we'll never

Smell the same
Creosote bush after rain
Is a small fact
I'm too tired to out ride.

*"Something / comes into the world unwelcome / calling disorder, disorder— //
If you hate me so much / don't bother to give me / a name: do you need / one more
slur / in your language, another / way to blame / one tribe for everything—"*

—LOUISE GLÜCK

Dear Catalpa,

Every time I write your name, say it in my mind, I feel I'm somehow
making you more real, as if each utterance were a breath into a bal-
loon expanding your little life. What's fucked up is how this phe-
nomenon also enlarges your passing. The more I feel your presence,
the more acute your absence is; the more of you I've got, the more
of you I've lost. Maybe that's why we were reluctant to acknowledge
your existence. You were our nameless secret. If we referred to you at
all, it was in abstractions like "the situation," or whispered between
us as "the pregnancy." But it was impossible pretending — name or
no name, you still were. More than just an inconvenience or morning sickness, you were a collision of cells, you had a heart, however
small, part mine, beating blood borrowed from the woman I love.

While I was feigning your nonexistence, I was simultaneously snooping out information about you on the internet. My search history looked something like, "how big is a fetus at 4 weeks," "when does fetus develop brain," "baby 8 weeks," "first heartbeat?" I quit one of these searches to pick up your mother from what she described as a "nightmare" shift at work. Picture her: her dominant right arm bound in an ugly beige sling velcroed to an immobilizer bound around her ribs, balancing plates of falafel and curried tofu on her left arm, refilling water glasses, mixing cocktails, the combined smells making her nauseous, excusing herself to the bathroom to barf up her breakfast of toast and turmeric tea. She never called in sick, not once. More impressive still, she managed to evade the curiosity and worry of her gossipy, but well-intentioned coworkers. Few people I've known can match her toughness and grace.

"Ingrid thinks I'm anemic," she said, as she dropped her body in the passenger seat.

"What did you say?" I said.

"I said I was hungover. I wish I was hungover! I can't believe a lima bean is causing all of this trouble," she said.

So it's the size of a lima bean, I thought. Aren't you glad that first name didn't stick? It wasn't until after you were gone that I secretly named you Catalpa.

On the evening of her appointment at Planned Parenthood, she told me the ultrasound technician told her your exact age. "Nine weeks, six days," she said. We scrolled back through the photos on my phone: cartoons we'd drawn, walks we'd taken in the prairie through sunflower and bee balm, fruits and fungi we'd foraged, meals cooked, sunsets viewed, fireworks, a video of a snail crawling over her hand. We came to the photos from the day nine weeks, six days ago, the day you were conceived. Where for so many days there'd been so many photos, on that day there was only one: a single close-up of a catalpa blossom.

Catalpas (*Catalpa bignonioides*) are thick-trunked deciduous trees sporting heart-shaped leaves through the summer and long seed pods that drip from their branches like green icicles each fall. I'll draw you a catalpa, but they really have to be seen, held, inhaled. They need to be seen in spring too, in full bloom. When St. Francis, in winter, asked a tree about the existence of God, the plant responded by erupting into bloom. The first time I read that, I assumed the saint had been communing with a catalpa. Catalpas bloom in these lush panicles, each blossom a funnel of white taffeta, a gown for a wood sprite, the petals painted with brushstrokes of wine-dark burgundy and saffron. Emily Dickinson dreamed her hands were bouquets of morning glories with carmines sprouting from her fingernails. If all my wishes weren't already tied up with her, I'd wish for catalpas to bloom from all of my fingers.

The day you were conceived, she and I walked hand in hand down the middle of the street through a tunnel of flowering catalpas. The blossoms littered the ground in such a way that one felt as if some vernal parade had just passed through. She wanted to pick some, but the flowers were high in the branches and out of reach, and those on the road were wilted and trampled.

"Guess it wasn't meant to be," she said.

On my way to visit her at work that night, I found another catalpa growing on the banks of a creek downtown near a bridge. When I leaned my torso over the railing I could just grip the petals. I harvested catalpa flowers until I filled an entire paper grocery sack. To this day, I can't think of many places I'd rather be than sitting across from her, eyes closed, head bowed, chest slowly rising as she breathes a bouquet of catalpas.

There was one light-hearted night before your conception when we discussed baby names in bed.

"Bones," she said. "Could you imagine being six and having 'Bones' written on your lunchbag? Sixty, and being named Bones? 'I want you to meet my husband, Mr. Bones.'"

"You'd hear the Jamaican nannies in Carroll Park calling out 'Thor, Honeysuckle! Get over here!'" I said.

"If we have a kid, who knows what we'll name it," she said. "But it'll be brilliant and hairy and gorgeous."

I was waiting, watching yellow birch leaves whirl in wind-blown eddies through the street while Johanna gathered her thoughts on the other end of the line.

"Okay, this is what you're going to do," she said. "First, the baby needs a name."

"I don't know how I feel about that," I said. "It feels wrong."

"Hear me out," she said. "Also, some sort of memorial. It doesn't have to be elaborate. Something quiet, something meaningful. Rituals are important."

A Friday afternoon, a month and a half after you were gone, I biked out to Lake MacBride by myself traversing the same roads we'd ridden the day of her accident. I sat in the ditch where she'd crashed, looking out past the palisades to a lake unmarred by wind. Two red-tailed hawks teetered on invisible thermals high in a pentimento sky. I leaned my bike against a tree, locked the tires, and trekked into the woods. The forest floor was a vault of rotting leaves and fallen trees. I found a huge hen of the woods, her favorite, but it was sagging and waterlogged. I clawed a few mushy handfuls from the mass and wrung them out in my fingers; an ochre juice dribbled out. And then I saw a huge puffball mushroom, a giant's skull nesting in the leaves. I dislodged it from the soil, severed its thin umbilical stem, and carried it off in my arms.

I hiked with it to a limestone cove on the lake shore where I laid the mushroom down in a bower of wood sorrel, fossilized coral, and purple asters. With my pocket knife I carved CATALPA in the puffball's soft flesh, followed by her last name, a hyphen, and then my last name. I crouched beside the memorial as the sun set in a rainbow-roll of vermillion, pink, and cornflower blue. I remained there for a while, reading and rereading your name as the evening overtook the day.

Night-Blooming Cereus

I'm never alone
> *With you living*
Inside me and every
> *Blossom and blade*
Of prairie grass I see
I see it for you
I see it for me.

THIRTEEN

AFTER MIDNIGHT ON MY LAST NIGHT in Tucson, we drove to Tohono Chul Park, the botanic gardens near the Whole Foods. Johanna had called that morning to say the night-blooming cereus might bloom after all. Tucsonians had been waiting for them to bloom since May.

"Renia de la Noche," said Sun. "This'll be my first time seeing them do their thing."

A pungent tropical rankness clung to the night wind. White Christmas lights seeped like mosses from the screwbean mesquites. People crept along the trails in silent clusters; there was a sense of being an interloper at some unknown religious observance, a foreign yet undeniably sacred rite. A pebble path opened onto a veranda where the arms of countless cereus cacti lolled in the gravel, their blooming heads staring up to the stars. The blossoms were enormous, waxy and white, each donning a corona of yellow stamens. Sharp green sepals radiated from the blooms in spiky collars. If you looked closely, you could see petals moving.

Sun crouched beside two flowers with his phone recording the blooming.

"As we watched / the slow unfolding of petals, there was a sense that maybe time / was more than a measure of decay," said Johanna.

I pricked my finger on one of the sepals, inhaled its scent.

Sun and Johanna were asleep. It was almost light in the foothills. The mountains materialized in mauve mounds against the violet dawn. I was out on the porch with a cup of the pu-erh I'd bought for her cooling on the table. Snorting and scratching came from the cacti and shrubs. I shined my headlamp revealing a family of javelinas, scuffling and rooting out bugs.

"That something lasts forever does not make it a thing of beauty, does not measure its worth," I wrote on the back of the horned lizard postcard I'd addressed to her. I also drew a pen and ink illustration of a night blooming cereus blossom.

"But just that it happens at all," I wrote. "Even for a little while."

ACKNOWLEDGMENTS

I have the best family, I am so outrageously unworthy of them. They are hilarious and strange and all of them lovers. My parents and siblings and dogs have sustained me through their love, all of my gratitude goes to them.

I would also like to offer gratitude to my many friends, loved ones, and fellow artists for their support. Thank you Wren Albertson-Rogers, Thomas Agran, Chris Ajello, Alonso Avilla, Pablo Balbotin-Rodriguez, Luther Bangert, Michael Barton-Sweeney, Matilda Bathhurst, Angad Bhai, Justin Boening, Barb Canin, Jesus Castillo, Dan Cesca, Sam Chang, Jed Cohen, Charlie D'Ambrosio, Daedalus, Max Davis, Benjamin Dohrmann, Casey Duffy, Barb Feathers, Leah Feygin, Finn, Mitch "Moody Marlin" Gardner, Andy Gates, Steph Gates, Matt Georges, Mike Gibisser, Hannah Givler, the Gnade Family, Shuja Haider, Rebecca Hanssens-Reed, Josh Haug, Traci Hercher, Cole Highnam, Jeff Holmes, Dr. Boris Igic, Alex Jimenez, Nimo Johnson, Riley Jonson, Betsy Kapp, Will Kapp, Colin Kostelecky, Kyle "Haunter" Miller, Fatima Mirza,

Matthew Moye, Greg Phillips, Andy Pilkington, Kristen Radtke, Nick Richards, Willa Richards, Mary Roach, Miigun Rotary, Ben Shattuck, Jess Smith, Kelly Smith, Marya Spence, Taylor Sperry, Alexa Stark, Lauren Struckmeyer, Stan Taft, Bryce Thornburg, Christine Utz, Dr. Jeffrey Valla, Kelsi Vanada, Stephanie Vaughn, Devon Walker, Liz Weiss, Sarabeth Weszely, Kipp Wettstein, Esther Williams, Liz Willis, Cammy York, Alycia Zieno, Nick "Shrimp" Zimmermann, Phil & Karen Zimmermann. Thank you Deb West. Thank you Anna Haglin.

I truly appreciate the friendship and generosity of Adam Levin and Camille Bordas. Thank you Adam for supporting this book in the ways you have, it means a great deal.

I am grateful for Pallas Athena Kate Christensen; thank you for your tireless encouragement and support of me as an artist, but really thank you for your tireless encouragement and support of me as a human being.

Ethan Canin has exceeded what it means to be a mentor, he has been a true friend; thank you for everything, E.

Thank you to Sarah Burnes and to the rest of the folks at the Gernert Company; thank you for standing by such a strange little book. And I pray every writer has the opportunity to experience something like the relationship I've had with my agent Andy Kifer. From the very first white hot and frayed first draft, Andy believed in this project and fought like a dog for it. So long as there are folks in the literature industry with Andy's quality of integrity and heart, there is still hope for art.

I want to thank John Knight; all folks who have had the privilege to know him have been better off for it.

Thank God for Curbside Splendor. Thank God for Cat Eves and Naomi Huffman. I can't imagine it is humanly possible for two individuals to work as hard on a book as these two have for this one. Cat has provided such unwavering and intimate care to this project all along the way and Naomi fought, line by line, draft by draft, to make this book the fullest realization of its aesthetic ambitions, what more could one hope for? Alban Fischer has done such beautiful work on this book, I am so proud of his contributions and grateful for his talents. Working together with these folks over the past year plus has been a beautiful dream.

Thanks to my students at Brooklyn Heights Montessori School, Iowa, and Cornell College. Thanks to Critical Hit Games, Little Village, Cornell College, *The Iowa Review,* Iowa Writers' Workshop, RDG Planning & Design, Sun Valley Writers' Conference, University of Iowa Campus Recreation and Wellness Center, El Paso Taqueria and Latin Market, Szechuan House, Prairie Lights, Agape Cafe, Columbus Junction, Dairy Queen, and Colonial Lanes.

I won't be the first to tell you that Karen Russell is a special person; she is so truly good, she is such a light. She is a genius of the heart, and she is funny as all hell. And she is humble, as proven by her penchant for gas station wine. A lot of people say things like, "if it weren't for so-and-so . . ." but I mean it when I say that if it weren't for Karen, you wouldn't be holding this book, I wouldn't be holding myself upright in my chair writing this. After you've weathered the maelstrom, you may look back and be surprised to see who was there with you through it all, keeping vigil and holding you in the light; many of the folks in this acknowledgement have been just that, and Karen chiefly among them. Thank you, K.

Each pump of my heart and breath in my lungs is a thank you to Jaime Gowans.

TIM TARANTO is a writer, visual artist, and poet from New York. His work has been featured in *Buzzfeed*, FSG's *Works in Progress*, *Harper's*, *The Iowa Review*, *McSweeney's Internet Tendency*, *Paris Review Daily*, the *Rumpus*, and *The Saint Ann's Review*. Tim is a graduate of Cornell University and the Iowa Writers' Workshop.